The 4MAT® System

Teaching to Learning Styles with Right/Left Mode Techniques

by Bernice McCarthy

Library of Congress
Catalog Card Number: 80-70421
Printed in the United States of America

This book was edited by Charles White and Mary
Colgan McNamara.
It was designed by Adrienne Rudy, Gary Gronlund,
and Dennis McCarthy.

Acknowledgements

The author wishes to thank the following for permission to reprint material included in this book:

The Chicago Tribune - New York News Syndicate, Inc. for the *Broom Hilda* Cartoon.

Report Card for the Other Side of the Brain excerpted from Brain/Mind Bulletin, published by Interface Press, Box 42211, Los Angeles, Calif. 90042; $15 a year. Send stamped, self-addressed business-size envelope for sample issue.

Farrar, Straus and Giroux, Inc. for "The Bridge Builder" from Rare Old Chums by Will Allen Dromgoole. Copyright by L. C. Page, now a division of Farrar, Straus and Giroux, Inc.

D. C. Heath and Company, Lexington, Mass. for student activity exercise in the Energy Unit.

Allyn and Bacon, Inc. Boston, Massachusetts for "Energy Saver's Checklist," "The Increasing Use of Electricity in the Home Checklist," and the "Electric Bill Checklist."

Contents

The 4Mat system is a model for teaching. It seems to work at all ages and with all subject matter. It is based on my belief that everyone can learn.

It began with my experience as a teacher. As of this summer, 1980, I have been a teacher for twenty-two years. I have taught all grades from kindergarten to college. I have also taught the handicapped. Although I have taken the last five years to step back and look at educational research, I remain first and foremost a school-teacher.

My goal these past five years has been to devise a teaching model that can be simply and efficiently used to improve the odds for students. The model presented in this book is the result of current research and the impatience I share with the students of today. In my teaching experience I have witnessed countless examples of lost or destroyed student potential. I have also seen young, enthusiastic teachers thrown into impossible teaching situations without the help, guidance, or support necessary to succeed. Those teachers who make it do so because of their creativity and their ability to live by their wits. perhaps this book will give them a running start.

The 4Mat System model is based on research from many fields. It includes findings in learning styles, right and left brain dominance, creativity, effective management, art, and movement/dance. It was conceived and developed as the result of a conference held in Chicago in December of 1979.

Two months earlier, while working on assorted research findings and thinking about my own experience with the diversities of how people learn, I outlined and classified the striking similarities found in the work of eighteen research-ers. These similarities seemed to have profound implications for educators. The classification system was sent to the researchers involved and simultaneously submitted to the McDonald Corporation. The people at McDonald's urged me to convene a conference which they agreed to fund. Eight researchers met to discuss the connections of our work and the possible ramifications of those connections for educators and trainers.

The conference was attended by myself and Dr. Joseph Bogen, Neurosurgery, Ross Loos Medical Center, Los Angeles; Dr. Jerre Levy, Behavioral Science, University of Chicago; Dr. Bill Bergquist, IBM Scientific Staff, Los Angeles; Dr. Betty Edwards, Art, California State University, Long Beach; Dr. David Kolb, Management, Case Western Reserve; Dr. Anthony Gregorc, Curriculum and Instruction, University of Connecticut; Dr. Louis Fisher, Education, University of Massachusetts; Dr. Barbara Fischer, Director of Smith College Campus School; Dr. Bill Hazard, Educational Administration, Northwestern University; Elizabeth Wetzig, Wetzig Dance Company, New York City; and Dennis Detzel, McDonald Corporation.

The conference was exhilarating. We spent three days exploring connections and asking questions.

- *Why were learning style researchers finding such striking similarities?*

- *How — if at all — were findings on right and left brain characteristics related to the learning style research?*

- *Could the techniques developed in art instruction be applied to other areas of the curriculum?*

- *Did the findings of our movement patterns relate to the four learning styles?*

- *How was math ability related to right or left brain dominance?*

- *Did the findings in right and left brain dominance in respect to sex relate to the success of female students in reading and the lack of success in male students?*

- *Can right mode dominant students succeed in left mode settings?*

- *What was the relationship between musical ability and math ability?*

- *What was the consensus of learning styles researchers about the right mode characteristic of concreteness and the left mode characteristic of abstractness?*

- *Could these diverse findings be applied to a teaching model?*

My heartfelt thanks to the people who attended that conference and to Bill Hazard of Northwestern and Dennis Detzel of McDonald's for making it possible.

And to the ten exciting people who attended that conference, I extend my gratitude for their time and interest and especially for their honesty.

This book is gratefully dedicated to them, and to the teachers of Johnsburg, Illinois, District 12, for using the model and teaching me so much.

Bernice McCarthy
Barrington Hills, Illinois
Summer, 1980

Much has happened since this book was first published. We have learned a great deal about 4MAT and its potential. We have also learned a great deal about teachers and teaching. And, most of all, we have learned about the strategies necessary for successful change.

4MAT in the Classroom

We have learned how to better look at 4MAT in process in the classroom, so we can more clearly estimate its impact. When teachers get involved in long-range 4MAT training (a year or more), the first thing that happens is their **attitudes** about learning shift:

they begin to believe in multiple kinds of intelligence,
they begin to honor diversity in their students' learning styles,
they begin to accept the task of motivating students as a primary responsibility,
they begin questioning the adequacy of student evaluation techniques.[1]

We found that expertise in 4MAT comes only after these significant attitudinal shifts occur.

We have also discovered a major curricula problem, the need to clarify the significant concepts in all content areas. Our current approach to content is topical rather than conceptual, based on discrete parts rather than significant ideas that connect and structure content.

Teachers, department chairs and curriculum coordinators need to learn to identify the significant concepts. We need to add the patterning skills to the outlining skills. We need to approach from the whole, then move to the parts. We have realized teachers need help to discover how to do this. We have begun to add strategies to our training seminars to assist teachers in these tasks.

Another stumbling block in writing a 4MAT unit or lesson is the inclusion of right-mode techniques. What are right-mode activities? Can anyone say, with any degree of certainty, that one kind of activity is right mode and another is left mode? No, **we cannot.**

We *can* say that certain kinds of processing favor the right mode: visuospatial, holistic, gestalt, subjective. Certain other kinds of processing favor the left mode: analytic, sequential, discrete, objective. We can firmly state that our students need both kinds of information processing. We need to honor both kinds of skills in our evaluation processes.

4MAT seems to be a catalyst for change, as it raises questions about:

meaning and connectedness of curricula, fragmentation in our approach to content, lack of emphasis on process, including the entire array of right-mode skills, and incomplete evaluation criteria, especially in the area of transferability and the creative use of content.

Teachers and Teaching

We have gained new respect for the teaching act itself. Successful teaching encompasses three major and very different areas of expertise:

*pedagogy, a knowledge of the nature of learners and learning

*content expertise, the extensive knowledge of a disipline and an equally important love for the content of that discipline, and

*orchestration, the personal presence necessary to orchestrate a group of students, with all the flow and flex necessary for successful timing, never outdistancing, never allowing stagnation.

As a result of our new understanding of the complexity of teaching, we are very concerned with the simplistic teacher evaluation techniques now in use and under consideration, including reductionist and mandated uses of 4MAT for such purposes.

Strategies for Successful Change

We discovered the primary way to help teachers enlarge their instructional techniques is peer coaching. And we found peer coaching seems to work best when teachers choose their own learning partners and when they are given in-school time for that process. We found the research showing principals as key to school excellence and school self-renewal to be absolutely true. Consequently we added increased administrative involvement to our training efforts.

And finally we've discovered that teachers are enormously interested in their profession. When teachers talk to other teachers about teaching, significant leaps in professionalism occur.

Many of our insights have come from our long-range projects. We thank them for their courage, not only in trying new things, but also for their patience and creativity as we learn together. We are very proud to be involved with them.

We cite the following schools and school districts for their exceptional professionalism, particularly for their willingness to share change strategies with each other.

Fairfax County Schools
Vienna, VA 22180
Dr. June Webb, Project Leader

Fisk Elementary School
Salem, NH 03079
Jane Batts, Project Leader

Hamilton-Wenham School District
South Hamilton, MA 01982
Janice Yelland, Project Leader

Kenmore-Town of Tonawanda Public Schools
Kenmore, NY 14223
Robert Freeland, Project Leader

Marion Community Schools
Marion, IN 46952
Carol Secttor, Project Leader

MSD of Lawrence Township
Indianapolis, IN 46226
Dr. Dwight Beall, Project Leader

North York Board of Education
North York, Ontario, Canada M2N 5N8
Jim Treliving, Project Leader

Putnam Public Schools
Putnam, CT 06260
Dr. Louise Pempek, Project Leader

Dr. Norman Bethune Collegiate Institute
Scarborough Board of Education
Agincourt, Ontario, Canada M1W 3G1
Dr. Brenda Shapiro, Project Leader

Seymour Heights Elementary School
North Vancouver, B.C. Canada V7H 1B8
Peter Beugger, Project Leader

Taunton Public Schools
Taunton, MA 02780
Sheilah McLaughlin and
Maureen Colton, Project Leaders

Upper Moreland School District
Willow Grove, PA 19090
Paul Mauger and
Becky Bride, Project Leaders

Windsor Public Schools
Windsor, CT 06095
Dr. Paul Sorbo, Project Leader

School Union #48
Wiscasset, ME 04578
Dr. Randy Collins, Project Leader

Yarmouth School Department
Yarmouth, ME 04096
Kerry Jones and
Ann Norment, Project Leaders

As 4MAT continues to develop and grow, it has become apparent to me that it is a catalyst for change. 4MAT is a kind of lens through which one can view teaching. It raises serious questions about the fragmentation of our approach to content. It provides a vocabulary useful for talking about what good teachers do when they teach. It provides them a repertoire of instructional methods, a cyclical context in which to place learning stages, and an appreciation of the diversity of learners.

Bernice McCarthy
Barrington, Illinois
Spring, 1987

Part One
Learning Styles

Chapter One

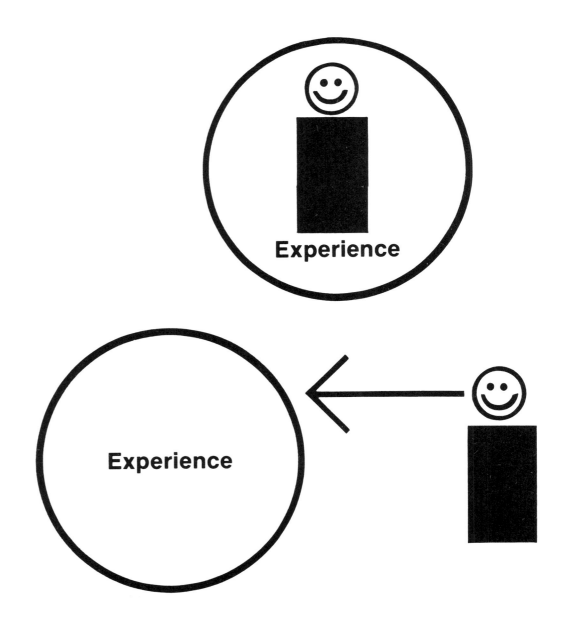

Learning Styles: What Are They?

People learn in different ways.

These differences
depend on many things:

who we are,
where we are,
how we see ourselves,
and what people ask of us.

There are two major differences
in how we learn.

The first is how we *perceive*,
the second is how we *process*.

We perceive reality differently.
We take things in in different ways.
In new situations,
some of us sense and feel our way,
while others think things through.

Those who perceive
in a sensing/feeling way
connect the experience,
the information, to meaning.
They learn through empathy,
through the lens of personhood.

Those who sense and feel
tend more to the actual experience itself.
They immerse themselves in the concrete reality.
They perceive through their senses.
They are intuitive.

And because personhood and intuition
are, by their very nature, holistic,
the process is essentially gestalt.

On the other hand,
those who think through the experience
tend more to the abstract dimensions of reality.
They analyze what is happening.
Their intellect makes the first appraisal.
They reason experience.
They perceive with a logical approach.

Whereas the feeling mode
is connected knowing,
the thinking mode is separate knowing.

Objectivity necessitates
a kind of standing outside,
an attempt to subtract
the personality of the perceiver
in order to take in the learning,
in order to be as free from bias as possible.

The particular perceiving orientation
you favor over time,
the feeling or the thinking,
is one of two major determinants
of your learning style.

3

We hover near different places on a continuum.

And our hovering place is our most comfortable place.

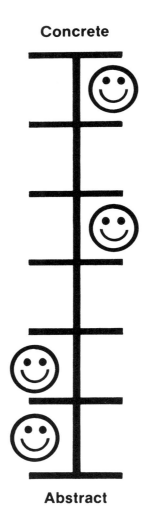

Concrete

Abstract

We hover near different places on a continuum
from concrete to abstract.

And the place where we hover
is our most comfortable place.

The sensor/feelers tend to be closer to the
concrete end of the line

and the thinkers tend to be closer to the abstract
end of the line.

Both kinds of perception are equally valuable.

*Both kinds have
their own strengths and weaknesses.*

Sensor/Feeler

Thinker

Concrete

Abstract

Schools do not value the sensing/feeling approach (except with very small children); therefore, it is neglected and sometimes downright discouraged.

Lovely for a thinker, sad and frustrating for a sensor/feeler.

The second major difference in how we learn
is
how we process experience and information
(how we make it part of ourselves).

As we perceive, we process.

Some of us   Others watch what's
jump right in   happening,
and try it.   reflect on it.

In processing experience and information,   Both kinds have their own
some of us are watchers,   strengths
while some of us are doers.   and
Both ways of processing information and   weaknesses.
experience are equally valuable.

Active   **Reflective**

Schools ask children to watch
and listen and reflect.
How lovely for a watcher,
how difficult for a doer.

Concrete

Abstract

The watchers
reflect on new things.
They filter them
 through their own experience
to create meaning connections.

The doers
act on new information immediately.
They reflect only after
they have tried it out.
In order to make it theirs,
they need to do it,
to extend it into their world.

Both kinds of
perceiving
(the concrete and the abstract)
are equally valuable,
and
both kinds of
processing
(reflective and active)
are equally valuable.

The particular way
each of us
perceives and processes
is the best way for us,
our most comfortable place.

Active ⊢⊢⊢⊢⊢ Reflective

There are some very good reasons why
schools don't value the different ways people
learn.

Take the sensing/feeling way of perceiving
and think about children.

Children are concrete, they sense and feel.

We are told they go to school to learn how to
think.

Somehow that need to teach them how to
think (a very important thing to do)
has become the *only* thing to do.

Also, the older we get, the more we
can abstract,
and be logical
and be rational.

That is very important for all of us,
sensors/feelers as well as thinkers.

Piaget found that we move through stages
in which we increase our ability
to be abstract.

The rise of civilization
is directly related to our ability
to be rational,
theoretical,
and abstract.

And so, teachers and parents try
to help their children
to grow up, to be more abstract.

**But learning is not all cognitive.
It is not all theoretical.
There is more to growing up
than increasing rationality.**

While it is very important to do,
it is not all there is.

Real education means more.

We need to learn to feel and think.

We need to honor both modes of perceiving.

We need also to refine the ability
to sense and feel,
to live in the concrete,
to deal with the real,
to understand the meaning.

Good business people do it.
Good artists do it.
Good politicians do it.
Good scientists do it.

The sensor/feelers need to refine
their intuitive gifts,
while also learning
to acquire the gifts of logic and analysis.

And the thinkers need to refine
their rational gifts,
while also learning
to trust the gifts of the senses,
their intuitive abilities.

We need to learn to reflect and act.

We need to honor both modes of processing.

Next, take the doing way
of processing experience
and think about schools.

Schools do some of the doing things.

Students read,
they write stories and essays
and sometimes poems,
they solve math problems,
they paint and draw,
they play music.
They do skills things,
they do workbooks.
(Notice that when the budget is cut, the doing
things are the first to go.)

But students don't experience the law,
and they don't experience their own history,
and they don't often get the chance to *be*
the person in the story.
(Sometimes good teachers give
 them the chance.)
They don't do science, except in rare lab
courses,
where they are not all expected
to arrive at the same results;
mostly they read about
and hear about
other people doing science.

They just don't get enough opportunities
to add their own egg.

That's because people are afraid,
especially administrators,
that when children do things,
they get noisy.

I find that odd,
because when I watch people
really engrossed in doing things,
they are usually very quiet.

I find it especially odd
because learning is interactive.
It is the learner
interacting with the learning
that is the real growth.

The processing dimension is a continuum
that ranges from the need to internalize
to the need to act,
from the specific personal fit
to manipulation and usefulness in the larger world.

Need to Act   **Need to Internalize**

Watchers need to refine
their reflective gifts,
while also developing the courage
to experiment and try.

And doers need to refine
their experimenting gifts,
while also developing the patience
to watch reflectively.

**To allow
and encourage
children to do
both
is to believe in
excellence.**

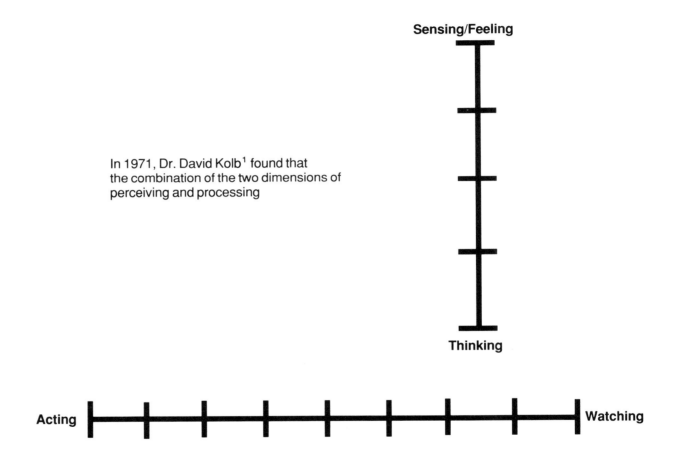

In 1971, Dr. David Kolb[1] found that the combination of the two dimensions of perceiving and processing

results in four different learning styles.

Concrete Experience
Kolb called the sensing/feeling dimension *Concrete Experience* and placed it at the top of this line, the vertical axis.

Active Experimentation
The doing dimension became *Active Experimentation* and was placed at the left end of the horizontal axis.

Reflective Observation
The watching dimension became *Reflective Observation* and was placed at the right end of this line, the horizontal axis.

Abstract Conceptualization
Kolb called the thinking dimension *Abstract Conceptualization* and placed it at the bottom of the vertical axis.

Kolb found that some people experience or
take in information
concretely, and they process
what they take in *reflectively*.

They are sensors/feelers and watchers.
Organizational development people
are like this.

So are social scientists.
They study life as it is lived –
through questionnaires, polls, or observation –
but then they reflect
about what they find.
They start with what they see,
then they generalize.
These people
fall in the top right-hand quadrant of his model.
Kolb calls them Divergers.

Kolb found that other people take in (perceive)
experience *abstractly*, and they process
what they take in *reflectively*.

These are the thinkers and watchers.
Research and design people are like this.

They start with an idea –
an abstraction –
then they reflect about it,
playing with it,
watching it take different shapes.
These people
fall in the lower right-hand quadrant of his model.
Kolb calls them Assimilators.

Kolb found that other people
take in experience *abstractly*
and then process what they take in *actively*.

They need to try things out for themselves,
they are thinkers and doers.
Engineers are like this.

They start with an idea,
then they try it out,
conduct experiments,
test it,
see if it works.
These people
fall into the bottom left-hand quadrant
of his model.
Kolb calls them Convergers.

And finally, Kolb found that some people
take in experience *concretely*
and process what they take in *actively*.

They are sensors/feelers and doers.
Marketing and sales people are like this.

They don't start with ideas,
but with what they
see, hear, touch, feel.
Then they plunge in
and try it out
in action.
These people
fall into the top left-hand quadrant of his model.
Kolb calls them Accommodators.

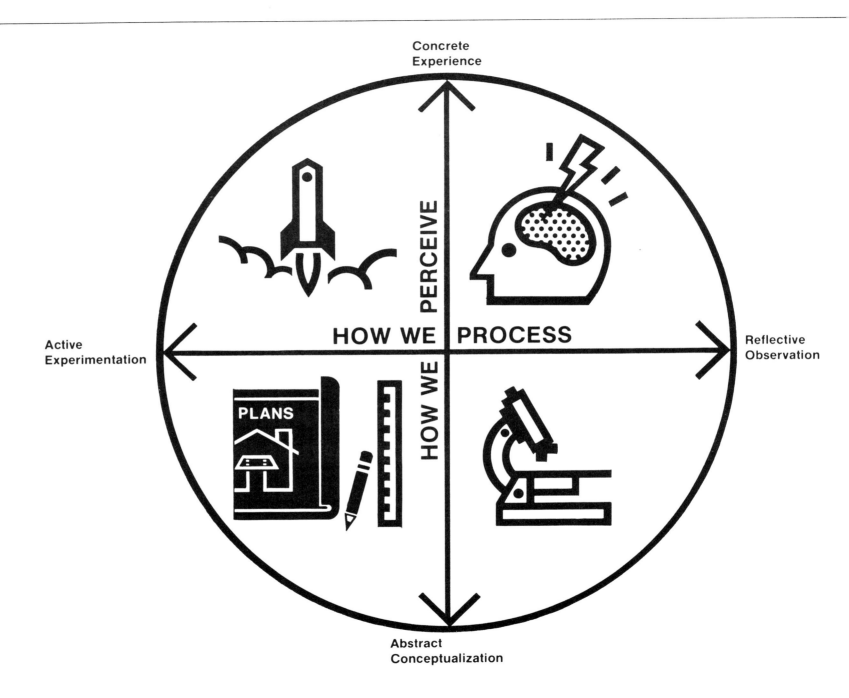

Concrete
Experience

PERCEIVE

HOW WE | PROCESS

Active
Experimentation

Reflective
Observation

HOW WE

PLANS

Abstract
Conceptualization

And so Kolb found that it is the combination of how we perceive and how we process that forms the uniqueness of our own learning style, our most comfortable way to learn.

Chapter Two

David Kolb's research represented a breakthrough because it formulated learning style findings into model form. But Kolb's contributions did not end with the model. He went on to analyze the different types of learners. He notes that our dominant learning abilities are the "result of our hereditary equipment, our particular past life experiences, and the demands of our present environment."[1] Here are brief descriptions of each learner identified by Kolb.[2]

Diverger

Concrete Experience
and
Reflective Observation

imaginative ability
gestalt (looking at the
whole, rather than the parts)
a people person
emotional
humanities and liberal arts
influenced by peers

Assimilator

Abstract Conceptualization
and
Reflective Observation

theoretical models
abstracts
(not interested in practical
use of theories)
a goal setting person
a systematic planner

Converger

Abstract Conceptualization
and
Active Experimentation

deductive
practical application of ideas
single correct answer
things rather than people
narrow interests
physical sciences
a goal setting person
a systematic planner

Accommodator

Concrete Experience
and
Active Experimentation

adaptive
intuitive, trial and error
relies on other people for
information
at ease with people
sometimes seen as impatient and pushy
technical and practical fields
influenced by peers

The findings of learning style researchers are strikingly similar. In fields ranging from psychology to management training, researchers have made nearly the same discoveries. Though they worked separately, with different techniques, in different areas, they came up with almost perfectly parallel learning schemes.

Whatever we look at, and however we look at it, we see it only through our own eyes.

In his book, <u>Psychological Types</u>[3,] Carl Jung explored the differences in the way people perceive and process information. He defined four categories.

Feelers
Feeling tells us the value of what is.

Feelers transfer value from themselves to what they experience. Thus they validate what happens to them and what they perceive in accord with emotions and not in accord with intellect. But this is a conscious process, since active feeling is a directed function, an act of the will. In a sense, it is rational, since values in general are assigned according to the laws of reason.

Thinkers
Thinking enables us to recognize the meaning of what is.

Thinkers are more classically rational. They engage in directed thinking. They arrange what happens and what they perceive into rational categories. This is a conscious act, in which judgment reviews and monitors the rational categories and their content.

Sensors
Sensation establishes what is.

Sensors perceive consciously. But they do not assign values to what they sense, like the Feeler, or fit it into categories like the Thinker. Rather, they are conscious but let the sensations happen without imposing control.

Intuitors
Intuition points to the possibilities of what might be.

Intuitors impose control on perceptions but in an unconscious way. Intuitors understand what they see and feel in a whole and complete way. They apprehend instinctively.

Gordon Lawrence

Based on the work of Isabel Myers, Lawrence describes sixteen different types of learners formed by the four dimensions of Carl Jung: Extravert to Introvert, a person's natural interests; Thinking to Feeling, a person's values and commitments; Sensation to Intuition, a person's preference for the concrete or the abstract; and Judgment to Perception, a person's work habits. The four basic types are listed below so the reader may compare them to the four major learning styles discussed in this book.[4]

Feeling Types

They tend to be very aware of other people and their feelings. They enjoy pleasing people, even in seemingly unimportant things. They need and love harmony. They often let their decisions be influenced by others. They are people-oriented and sympathetic.

Thinking Types

They do not readily show emotion. They analyze and put things into logical order. They tend to make decisions impersonally. They are sticklers about being treated fairly. They are firm-minded.

Sensing Types

They like established ways of doing things and usually reach conclusions step-by-step. They tend to be good at precise work and work more steadily when time lines are predetermined. They are patient with details.

Intuitive Types

They like solving new problems. They reach conclusions quickly. They follow their inspirations, good or bad. They work in bursts of energy, with slack time in between. They are patient in complicated situations.

Simon and Byram also adapted Jung's work and formed the following descriptions of four student types.[5]

The Feeler Student

Is helpful, sensitive, and expressive. Is creative and artistic. Likes hearing about and expressing feelings. S/he feels intensely and tends to overpersonalize. Personal meaning is extremely important.

The Thinker Student

Is organized, accurate and detailed. Is systematic and likes structure. Is logical and time-conscious. Tends to be overly critical. Worries about being perfect. Really loves to figure things out.

The Sensor Student

Is an initiator, gets things going. Is practical and productive. Organizes learning around activities. Is impatient and tends to interrupt. Has an energetic nature. Loves to keep active.

The Intuitor Student

S/he brings different points of view together. Is interesting and inventive. Looks for underlying principles. What "might be" is more important than "what is." Loves the big picture.

David Keirsey and Marilyn Bates are trainers of therapists and diagnosticians of dysfunctional behavior at California State at Fullerton.

They have written a useful book, *Please Understand Me: Character and Temperament Types.*

In this book, the Jung-Meyers typology is explained and presented using the four "temperaments" as a basis for the types.

"One's temperament is that which places a signature or thumbprint on each of one's actions, making it recognizably one's own."

Apollo — commissioned to give man a sense of spirit

Prometheus — to give men science

Epimetheus — to convey a sense of duty

Dionysus — to teach man joy

Hippocrates' temperaments, the work of Spranger, Adler and others are compared and contrasted in this highly readable book.

The work contains many insights into learning types and even includes a section on teaching styles.

David Merrill of Personnel Predictions,[7] a Denver-based firm, is in the field of management training. His work on classifying "social styles" is of great value to educators. Dr. Merrill's descriptions have evolved over twenty years of study.

Merrill has a construct for "social effects of behavior patterns" that covers a spectrum of possible responses. From this construct he has evolved the four descriptions seen below. Merrill also adds the dimension of "versatility" to his model. He defines versatility as social resourcefulness: the awareness, sensitivity, and appropriateness of individual social responses requiring input from several people familiar with the individual in more than one circumstance.

His work deserves to be carefully considered by anyone interested in furthering teacher awareness of the differences among students as well as those concerned with increasing teacher flexibility.

Driver

Pushy	Strong willed
Severe	Independent
Tough	Practical
Dominating	Decisive
Harsh	Efficient

Expressive

Manipulative	Ambitious
Excitable	Stimulating
Undisciplined	Enthusiastic
Reacting	Dramatic
Egotistical	Friendly

Amiable

Conforming	Supportive
Unsure	Respectful
Pliable	Willing
Dependent	Dependable
Awkward	Agreeable

Analytical

Critical	Industrious
Indecisive	Persistent
Stuffy	Serious
Picky	Exacting
Moralistic	Orderly

Valerie Hunt is an author, educator, and founder of The Creative Movement Laboratory at UCLA in 1967. Hunt's identification of four "body tension" patterns is striking in its relationship to learning style research.[8]

Assister

Absorbs reality.
Type awareness = absorption or oneness with reality (stream of consciousness)
Moving-thinking element = flow/direction

Posturer

Forms reality.
Type awareness = form or process of ordering reality (eliminating and reordering reality)
Moving-thinking element = shape

Resistor

Edits reality.
Type awareness = objectification or the naming of reality (editing what one sees, hears, tastes, touches, feels, or measures)
Moving-thinking element = thrust

Percerverator

Enriches reality.
Type awareness = coloring or the enriching of reality from self (embellishing or weighing words and concepts)
Moving-thinking element = weight

My own work grew out of a six-year experiment at a suburban Chicago high school. The learning styles I classified are strikingly similar to the findings of the other researchers.[9]

Type One Learner

Seeks personal meaning. Judges things in relationship to values. Functions through social interaction. Wants to make the world a better place. Is cooperative and sociable. Respects authority, when it is earned.

Type Two Learner

Seeks intellectual competence. Judges things by factual verification. Functions by adapting to experts. Needs to know "the important things," and wants to add to the world's knowledge. Is patient and reflective. Prefers chain-of-command authority.

Type Three Learner

Seeks solutions to problems. Judges things by their usefulness. Functions through kinesthetic awareness. Wants to make things happen. Is practical and straightforward. Sees authority as necessary, but will work around it if forced.

Type Four Learner

Seeks hidden possibilities. Judges things by gut reactions. Functions by synthesizing various parts. Enjoys challenging complacency. Is enthusiastic and adventuresome. Tends to disregard authority.

It is evident that researchers from diverse fields are identifying similar strands. Running through the different descriptions of perceiving and processing are many of the same conceptual insights. One way to see how similar they are is to summarize their findings by overlaying them on the model developed by Kolb. I want to make it very clear to the reader at this point that these connections are my own. As I studied the work of these researchers, the similarity of their results struck me and corroborated my insights and findings about student differences. In some instances, as is the case with any overlay, the correspondences are approximate rather than exact.

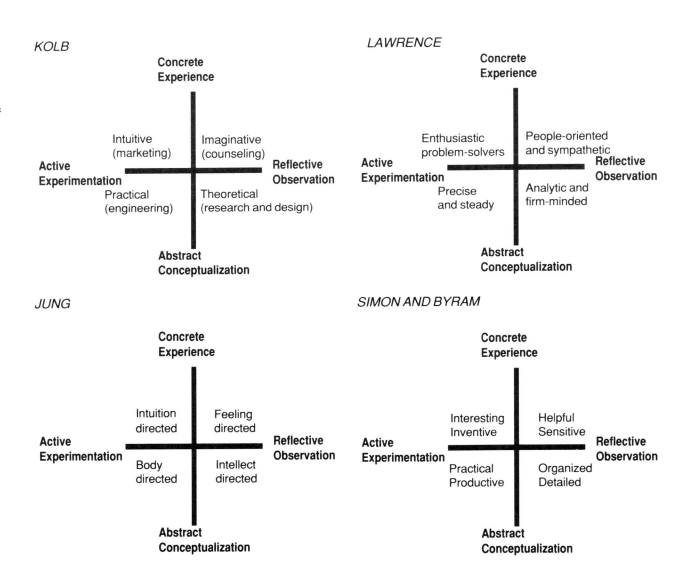

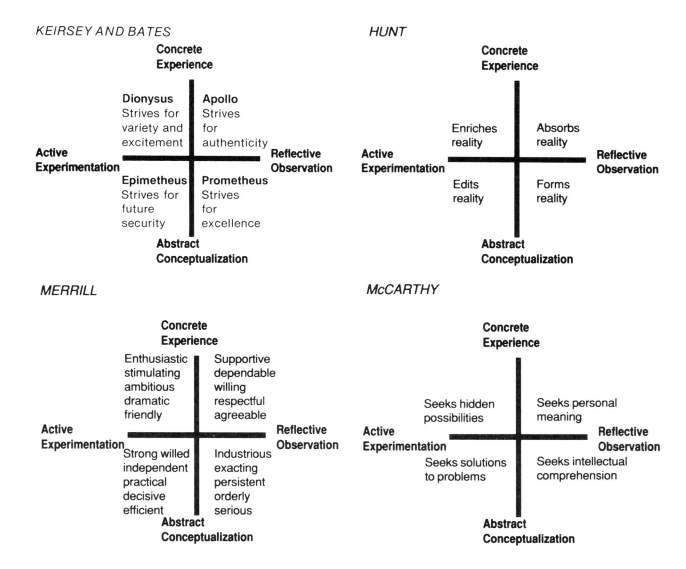

KEIRSEY AND BATES

Concrete
Experience

Dionysus
Strives for
variety and
excitement

Apollo
Strives
for
authenticity

Active
Experimentation

Reflective
Observation

Epimetheus
Strives for
future
security

Prometheus
Strives
for
excellence

Abstract
Conceptualization

HUNT

Concrete
Experience

Enriches
reality

Absorbs
reality

Active
Experimentation

Reflective
Observation

Edits
reality

Forms
reality

Abstract
Conceptualization

MERRILL

Concrete
Experience

Enthusiastic
stimulating
ambitious
dramatic
friendly

Supportive
dependable
willing
respectful
agreeable

Active
Experimentation

Reflective
Observation

Strong willed
independent
practical
decisive
efficient

Industrious
exacting
persistent
orderly
serious

Abstract
Conceptualization

McCARTHY

Concrete
Experience

Seeks hidden
possibilities

Seeks personal
meaning

Active
Experimentation

Reflective
Observation

Seeks solutions
to problems

Seeks intellectual
comprehension

Abstract
Conceptualization

Learning Style Characteristics

The following descriptions represent the major findings of the learning style researchers just discussed.

Type One:
The Imaginative Learners

As **learners** they perceive information concretely and process it reflectively.
They integrate experience with the self. They learn by listening and sharing ideas.
They are imaginative thinkers who believe in their own experience.
They excel in viewing direct experience from many perspectives. They value insight thinking.
They work for harmony. They need to be personally involved. They seek commitment.
They are interested in people and culture. They are thoughtful and enjoy observing others.
They absorb reality. They seek meaning and clarity.

As **teachers** they are interested in facilitating individual growth.
They try to help people become more self-aware.
They believe curricula should enhance the ability to be authentic.
They see knowledge as growth in personal insight and encourage authenticity in their students.
They like discussions, group work, and realistic feedback about feelings.
They are caring people who seek to engage their students in cooperative efforts.
They are aware of social forces that affect human development.

They are able to focus on meaningful goals.
They tend to become fearful under pressure and sometimes lack daring.

As **leaders** they thrive on developing good ideas, even though this is very time-consuming.
They tackle problems by first reflecting alone and then brainstorming with staff.
They exercise authority with trust and participation.
They work for organizational solidarity.
They need staff who are supportive and share their sense of mission.

Strength:	Imaginative ideas
Function by:	Value clarification
Goals:	To be involved in important issues and to bring harmony
Careers:	Counseling, teaching, organizational development, humanities and social sciences
Favorite Question:	Why?

Type Two:
The Analytic Learners

As **learners** they perceive information abstractly and process it reflectively.

They devise theories by integrating their observations into what is known.

They seek continuity. They need to know what the experts think.

They learn by thinking through ideas. They form reality. They value sequential thinking. They need details.

They critique information and collect data. They are thorough and industrious.

They will re-examine the facts if situations perplex them.

They enjoy traditional classrooms. They find ideas fascinating.

They prefer to maximize certainty and are uncomfortable with subjective judgments.

They seek intellectual competence and personal effectiveness.

As **teachers** they are interested in transmitting knowledge.

They try to be as accurate and knowledgeable as possible.

They believe curricula should further understanding of significant information and should be presented systemically.

They see knowledge as deepening comprehension. They encourage outstanding students.

They like facts and details and organized sequential thinking.

They are traditional teachers who seek to imbue a love of knowledge.

They believe in the rational use of authority. Sometimes their dominating attitude tends to discourage creativity.

As **leaders** they thrive on assimilating disparate facts into coherent theories.

They tackle problems with rationality and logic.

They lead by principles and procedures.

They exercise authority with assertive persuasion and by knowing the facts.

They work to enhance their organization as an embodiment of tradition and prestige.

They need staff who are well organized, write things down with diligence and care, and follow through on agreed decisions.

Strength:	Creating concepts and models
Function by:	Thinking things through
Goals:	Intellectual recognition
Careers:	Mathematics, research and planning, natural sciences
Favorite Question:	What?

Type Three:
The Common Sense Learners

As **learners** they perceive information abstractly and process it actively.

They integrate theory and practice. They learn by testing theories and applying common sense.

They are pragmatists. They believe if it works, use it. They are down-to-earth problem-solvers, who resent being given answers. They do not stand on ceremony but get right to the point.

They have a limited tolerance for fuzzy ideas.

They value strategic thinking.

They are skills oriented. They experiment and tinker with things.

They need to know how things work. They edit reality, cut right to the heart of things.

Sometimes they seem bossy and impersonal. They seek utility and results.

As **teachers** they are interested in productivity and competence.

They try to give students the skills they will need to be economically independent in life.

They believe curricula should be geared to this kind of focus.

They see knowledge as enabling students to be capable of making their own way.

They encourage practical applications. They like technical things and hands-on activities.

They are exacting and seek quality and productivity.

They believe the best way is determined pragmatically.

They use measured rewards.

They tend to be inflexible and self-contained and lack team-work skills.

As **leaders** they thrive on plans and time lines. They tackle problems by making unilateral decisions. They lead by personal forcefulness, inspiring quality. They exercise authority by reward/punishment. (The fewer the rules the better but enforce rigorously the ones you have.) They work hard to make their organization productive and solvent.

They need staff who are task-oriented and move quickly.

Strength:	Practical application of ideas
Function by:	Factual data gathered from hands-on experiences
Goals:	To bring their view of the present in line with future security
Careers:	Engineering, applied sciences, surgeons
Favorite Question:	How does this work?

Type Four:
The Dynamic Learners

As **learners** they perceive information concretely and process it actively.

They integrate experience and application. They learn by trial and error.

They are believers in self-discovery. They are enthusiastic about new things.

They are adaptable, even relish change. They excel when flexibility is needed.

They often reach accurate conclusions in the absence of logical justification.

They are risk takers who are at ease with people.

They enrich reality by taking what is and adding something of themselves to it.

They are sometimes seen as manipulative and pushy.

They seek to influence.

As **teachers** they are interested in enabling student self-discovery.

They try to help people act on their own visions.

They believe curricula should be geared to learners' interests.

They see knowledge as a tool for improving the larger society.

They encourage experiential learning. They like variety in instructional methods.

They are dramatic teachers who seek to energize their students.

They attempt to create new forms, to stimulate life and to draw new boundaries.

They tend to rashness and manipulation.

As **leaders** they thrive on crisis and challenge.

They tackle problems by looking for patterns, scanning possibilities.

They lead by energizing people.

They exercise authority by holding up a vision of what might be.

They work hard to establish their organizations as front runners.

They need staff who can follow up and implement details.

Strength:	Action and presenting challenges
Function by:	Acting, testing and creating new experiences
Goals:	To bring action to ideas
Careers:	Marketing, sales, entertainment, education, social professions
Favorite Question:	What if?

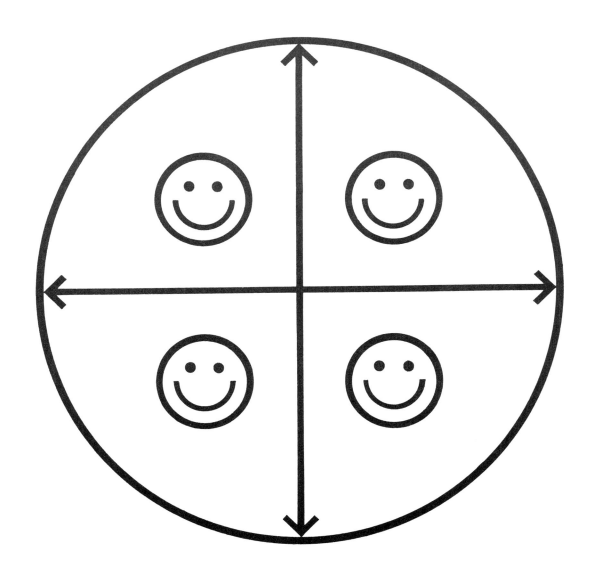

All four styles of learning
are equally valuable.
Each has its own
strengths
and
weaknesses.
If you're
Type
   One,
      Two,
         Three,
            or Four,
that is the most comfortable place for you to be.
That is your best learning style.

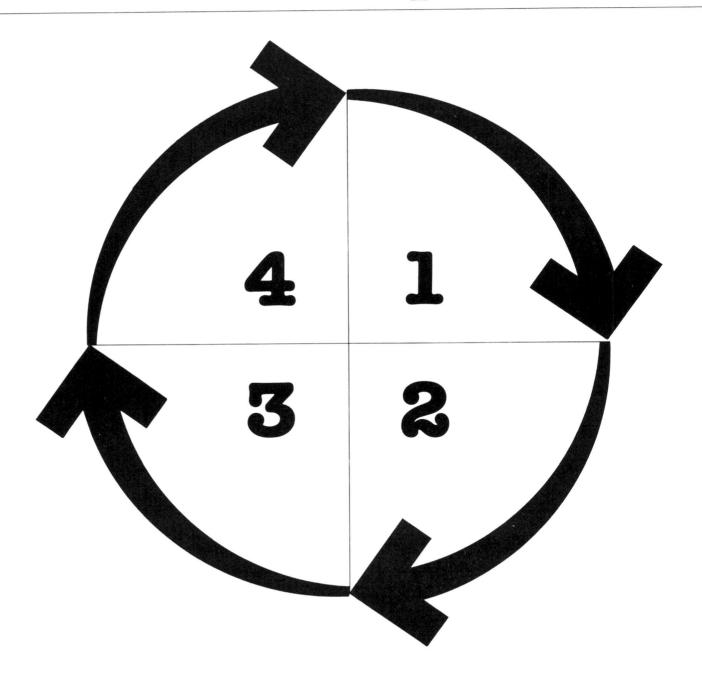

Chapter Three

Kolb's model is important not only because he has given us parameters for classifying different learning styles, but also because the model presupposes an organic sequence of learning from experience to reflection to conceptualization to experimentation.

All students get a chance to shine 25% of the time.

Visualize the circle as a clock. Students begin at 12 o'clock
with Concrete Experience.
By moving clockwise around the circle, they next develop the skills of Reflective Observation.
From that point students move to Abstract Conceptualization
and finally to Active Experimentation.

Then the cycle begins again, with new, richer experiences in ever-widening spirals.

In this way, all students,
whatever their learning styles,
get a chance to "shine" 25% of the time.
That is not possible in most schools today.
Only the Twos get the kind of teaching they need. The other three types are expected to learn in the Two Mode.

PLANS

48

I maintain that this is a natural learning
progression.
We all need to learn to "move around the circle."

We sense and feel, we experience,
    then we watch, we reflect,
        then we think, we develop theories,
      we conceptualize,
          then we try out our theories,
        we experiment.
Finally, we apply what we have learned to the
next similar experience.
We get smarter, we apply experience to
experience.

*Remember each of the four learning style types
has a quadrant
where s/he is most comfortable,
where success comes easily.*

The Imaginative Learners, those who fall in
Quadrant One,
prefer to learn by sensing/feeling and watching.

The Analytic Learners, those who fall in
Quadrant Two,
prefer to learn by thinking and watching.

The Common Sense Learners, those who fall in
Quadrant Three,
prefer to learn by thinking and doing.

And the Dynamic Learners, those who fall in
Quadrant Four,
prefer to learn by sensing/feeling and doing.

The most important thing to remember
is that all of the learners
need all of the cycle.

The cycle is more important
than any one segment.

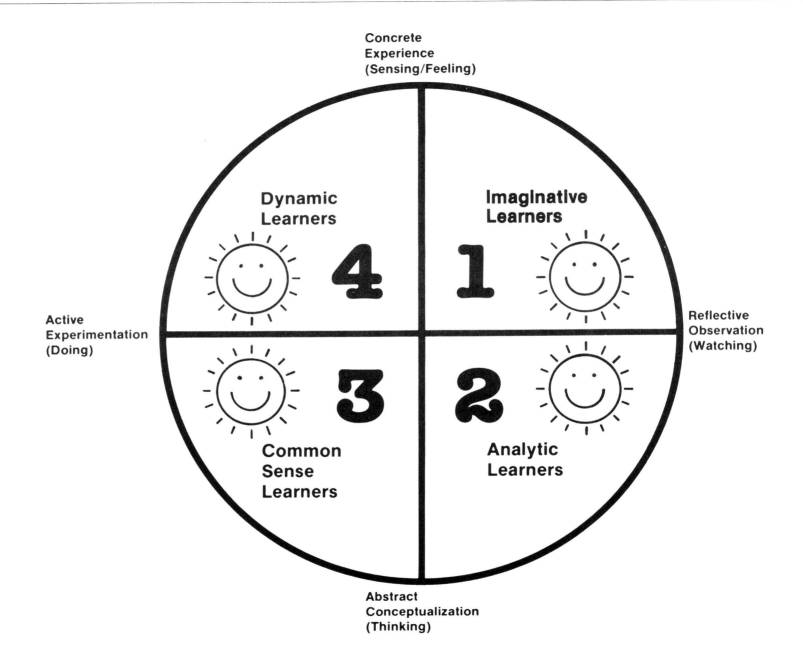

Concrete
Experience
(Sensing/Feeling)

Dynamic
Learners

4

Imaginative
Learners

1

Active
Experimentation
(Doing)

Reflective
Observation
(Watching)

3

Common
Sense
Learners

2

Analytic
Learners

Abstract
Conceptualization
(Thinking)

Schools validate the way Type Twos learn.

About 70% of our learners are *not* Type Twos.

When someone is teaching us
in our most comfortable style,
we learn.
But more importantly,
we feel good about ourselves.

Analytic Learners, those who fall in the second
quadrant, succeed in school.
School validates the way they learn.
Not so with the other three learning styles.

According to available data, about 70% of our
students are *not* Analytic Learners.

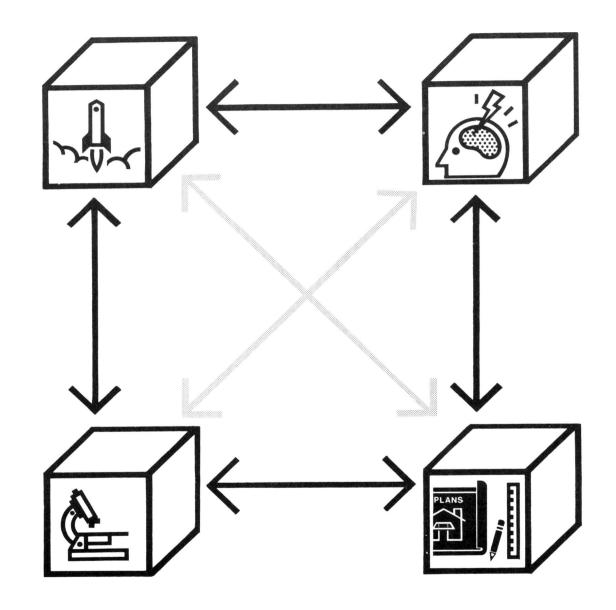

If 70% of our students learn most comfortably in
ways not generally attended to in our schools,
how should we proceed?

Should we identify their most comfortable style
and teach only to that strength?

If we divide our students into four groups,
and teach them only *their* way,
they will be very good in their own quadrants…
but they will not develop other learning skills.

If the Ones, the Imaginative Learners, learn only
how to refine their natural gifts
of experiencing and reflecting…
they will lack the necessary ability to analyze
and try out what they figure out.

If the Twos, the Analytic Learners, learn only
how to refine their natural gifts
of conceptualizing and reflecting …
they will lack the common sense
that comes from doing and experiencing.

If the Threes, the Common Sense Learners,
learn only
how to refine their natural gifts
of conceptualizing and experimenting…
they will lack the ability to experience life and
reflect on what they have learned.

If the Fours, the Dynamic Learners, learn only
how to refine their natural gifts
of experiencing and experimenting…
they will lack the organizational skills
that come with analysis and reflection.

It seems paradoxical,
but when we feel good about the way we learn,
when we succeed in what we try,
we start paying attention to how other people
learn.

We begin reaching into other styles.

The process of learning
that best actualizes development,
the kind of learning that best aids real growth,
requires interaction that confronts and resolves.
It requires movement from
concrete to abstract,
from reflective to active.
It requires movement through the entire cycle.

Such is the nature of humanness,
to adapt:
adaptation between the learner and the learning,
between the self and the group,
between actual development and potential
development.

Of such processes,
meaning is made.

It is the interaction
between the learner and the learning
that is the thing.

People both create themselves
and are created by their experience
through the choices they make
and the resulting patterns created by those
choices.

And the movement through the major learning style dimensions is the very stuff of the learning process itself.

Therefore,
the 4MAT System teaches in all four ways:
from experience,
    to reflection,
        to conceptualization,
            to experimentation
and back to experience.

If you use the 4MAT System when you teach,
each of the four learning types will get his/her chance to shine.
Each of the four learning types will know you believe in his/her uniqueness.

Love and trust mean
paying attention to the uniqueness of others.

I'm OK and you're OK means
we're not defensive or fearful
about who we are.
When we like ourselves,
we become open to the way other people are.
Then we can learn from them.

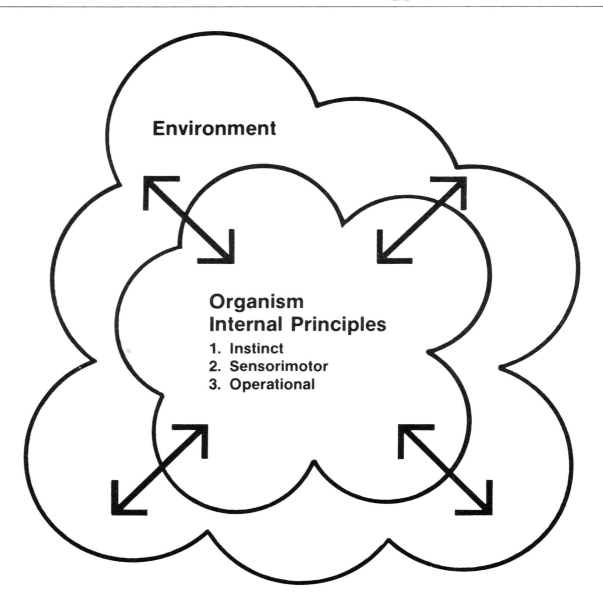

Chapter Four

Environment

Organism
Internal Principles
1. Instinct
2. Sensorimotor
3. Operational

The Ladder and The Cycle

Piaget[1] studied how thinking is developed. He approached his study as a biologist.

Every living organism contains its own biological structure. This *living* structure stands in *active* relationship to its environment and has knowledge of that environment. Piaget's use of the term "knowledge" is broader than mere intellectual knowledge and includes certain internal principles which manifest themselves behaviorally. These regulate how an organism functions with its environment. In other words, the internal structure and the external function are two sides of the same coin.

Piaget identified three levels of internal principles which regulate how an organism functions with its environment, three levels of "knowing".

1. rhythmic, reflex-like regulations of *instinctual* structures.
2. action-oriented regulations of *sensorimotor* structures.
3. "intelligent" regulation of *operational* structures.*

All three levels are part of all human knowledge. There are no neat separations, since they overlap in many instances.

*An interesting contrast can be made to Paul MacLean's Triune Brain: the reptilian complex, the limbic system, and the neocortex·[2]

Piaget:
Age-related regularities in reasoning processes

Knowing

Formal Operational
12-15 years

Concrete Operational
7-11 years

Preoperational
(Representational)
2-6 years

Sensorimotor
0-2 years

Kegan: (on Piaget)
The Evolving Self [3]

To Integrate.
(Emerging from embeddedness, to better relate, to reintegrate)

Reflecting on one's own thinking. From actual to possible, "what is" is only a piece of "what might be". Generalizability

Embedded in the concrete. Learning engaged with physical dimensions, the logic of classes and relations.

Embedded in the perceptions. Life is a series of encounters. Images of the world played with and manipulated.

Embedded in the reflexes. Learning through feeling, touching, handling. Movement toward experimental, exploratory.

Piaget's Levels (The Ladder)

Piaget studied the developmental nature of human intelligence. He found that growth toward abstract reasoning is a series of age-related stages.

Learners move from activities embedded in the reflexes (feeling, touching, handling) to being captivated by the divergence of the world as seen in images to be manipulated.

Learners then turn to the concreteness of classifying and relating the physical things of the world, and finally they move on to formal thinking.

Formal thinking includes:
*making hypotheses that can be expressed as premises offered for debate,
*leaving the real to invent the imaginary, and
*becoming conscious of one's own thinking.

Piaget's ladder shows that as we grow we develop scientific rationality.

This is the point in Piaget's work where many theorists and educators stop. Piaget himself never stopped there. His essential genius, according to Kegan, lies in his loyalty to "the ongoing conversation between the individuating organism and the world."[4]

In addition to Piaget's different levels of development,
there are different **ways** people develop.
There are different learning styles.

We are suggesting that development is four dimensional.
We develop higher values and meanings,
we develop deeper conceptual connections,
we develop more problem-solving skills,
and we develop more ability to create anew as we meld ourselves and our unique experiences to what we learn.

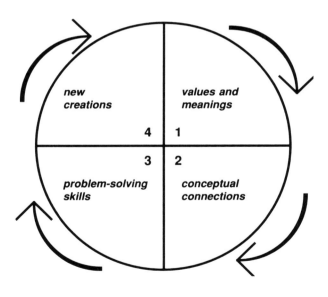

In other words,
we develop in all four quadrants,
and some of us do better in some quadrants than others.

The Type One Learners learn best through sensing/feeling and reflecting.
The Type Two Learners learn best through conceptualizing and reflecting .
The Type Three Learners learn best through conceptualizing and experimenting.
The Type Four Learners learn best through experiencing and experimenting.

Each learning style has a favorite way of going up Piaget's Ladder.
But all learners need to experience the entire cycle.

So we must stop focusing only on the ladder.
We must also attend to the cycle.

Learning is a continuous process
grounded in experience.
Knowledge is continuously
interacting with experience.
Equal emphasis is placed
on the cycle and
the stages of development.
Educators have focused on Piaget's
age-related stages
(The Ladder)
and neglected the process
(The Cycle) .

Educators have accorded the
reflective and the abstract processes
higher honors than the concrete
and the active.

Type Two Learners are
not at higher stages of development
because they prefer the separate
knowing of theory over the connected
knowing of experience.

We have misunderstood the meaning
of **concrete.**

Many have taken Piaget's concrete step
(the pre-abstract), which is a stage in
cognition where one begins to
cognitively see and manipulate the
physical world, and confused it with
the real, felt gusto and earnestness
of whole knowing, affective, gestalt
and individually unique.

We have misapplied a definition of
a cognitive step
(albeit a most necessary one)
to a process of knowing that is
the very lens of personhood itself.
Somehow the concrete and active
dimensions of knowing have been
neglected. Yet without the concrete,
without the real,
what is there to abstract about?

We have also dishonored the doing
dimension of processing in favor of
the reflecting dimension of processing.

Manipulating learning,
tinkering with what we are shown,
experimenting with what the experts say—
these processes transfer
learning to our own lives,
to the places where we live,
so we can integrate them.

By honoring the Type Two
Learners above others,
we structure our learning institutions
to lavish emphasis on
narrow and incomplete
definitions of thinking.

We have made the map the territory
and named map-knowing
a higher form of intellect
than territory-knowing.

Real scientific rationality stands in
service to whole knowing.
It does not exist apart from it.

And there are diverse ways to achieve
all the higher levels of knowing.
We go up these ladders
with different learning styles.
We develop higher abilities
to symbolize, to reflect, to act and
to feel.
And we do this by different means.

The exclusive focus on the abstract
and the reflective
has resulted in a false dichotomy,
a dichotomy between
what minds think and what bodies feel.

I propose that we look at stages of
learning as a cycle as well as a ladder.
Teachers need to "go around the circle"
as they take their students to more
encompassing levels of valuing,
observing and experimenting,
as well as in conceptualizing.

We need to allow students to function
with their innate gifts as a focus,
a home base,
while they work with other students
who have different styles
which are honored in turn.

We need to combine the ladder
and the cycle.

The Cycle itself is the learning process.

The movement around the 4MAT cycle
is the very stuff of the learning process itself.

The movement is from experiencing
to reflecting,
   to conceptualizing,
      to tinkering and problem-solving,
         to integrating new learning into the self.

The movement involves a constant
balancing and rebalancing
between
being in experience and analyzing experience,
between subjective and objective,
between connected and separate,
between being and knowing.

From connectedness to separation, back to
connectedness, to separation, back to
connectedness to separation, back to…
…from "in here" to "out there."

Kegan describes it this way:
"The adaptive conversation is the very source of,
and the unifying context for, thought and
feeling;…
this process is about the development of
'knowing.'"[5]

When we experience something new,
we are initially immersed in it,
simply because we approach newness
with our whole selves.
We are **subject**ive about it.
We are **subject**ed to it.
We apprehend it, capture it
in the web of our meaning.

We have connected to it.

But almost immediately we begin the
process of filtering the experience.
We filter it through who and what we are,
what our past has brought us to
in this moment.
We internalize newness through
our subjective "feel filter".
We experience newness in the scheme of our
personal world.

As we begin this process we emerge
from embeddedness in the "thing"
to a separation from it.

We begin to release ourselves from being
subjective and personal about
the learning so we can really begin
to look at it objectively.

Learning is the making of meaning.

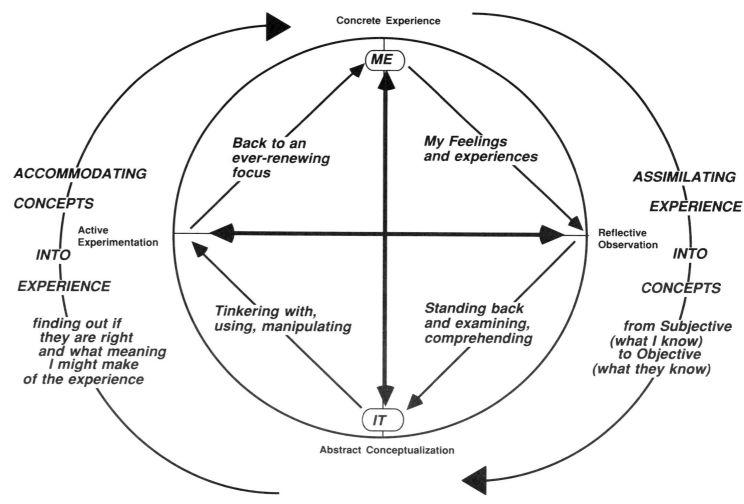

Concrete Experience

ME

Back to an
ever-renewing
focus

My Feelings
and experiences

ACCOMMODATING

CONCEPTS

Active
Experimentation

INTO

EXPERIENCE

*finding out if
they are right
and what meaning
I might make
of the experience*

*Tinkering with,
using, manipulating*

*Standing back
and examining,
comprehending*

ASSIMILATING

EXPERIENCE

Reflective
Observation

INTO

CONCEPTS

*from Subjective
(what I know)
to Objective
(what they know)*

IT

Abstract Conceptualization

This separation is necessary
in order to really see it,
in order to be **object**ive about it.
We deal with our feelings and
move through them.

We begin then to see the learning
as object---
as something interesting,
something curious,
something that intrigues us cognitively.

We have separated ourselves from it.

We symbolize it by naming it.
We look at what others say about it,
what others have done with it, and
where it fits in the scheme of the larger world.
We comprehend it.

But comprehension is not enough.
We must try it, tinker it,
play with it, watch it work, and make it work,
we must do it.
Now that it has become the object,
we must become the object manipulator.

We interact with it,
we change it to suit us,
we use it,
we enrich it
and are enriched by it.

We place it in our world,
we transfer it to where we live.
We integrate it.

The movement from embeddedness,
from being subjective (personally involved)
to being objective (separate and cognitive)
is necessary.
It is necessary to stand away
in order to understand,
in order to take back,
in order to really know.

The separation prepares the way for the learner
to relate anew to what is being learned…
so s/he can go around the cycle to newer, richer
experience.

One needs to relate anew to what one is learning
in order to ultimately integrate into the self,
in order to make meaning.

The making of meaning, which is learning, is in
and out——
into the self
and out to the world——
over and over again.

And so the 4MAT cycle is more important than
any one segment.
The movement around the circle includes all
learners,
engaging them and stretching them,
while leading them to expertise in multiple ways
of learning.

The movement is a constant balancing from subject to object and back again.

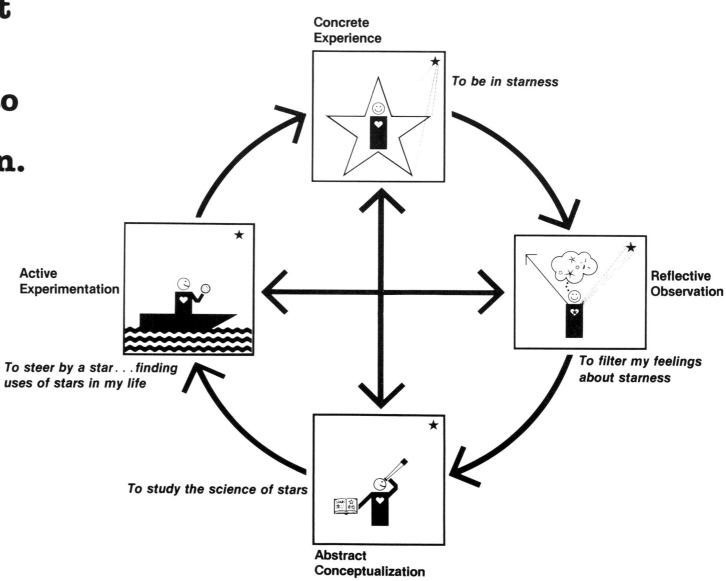

Concrete Experience

To be in starness

Reflective Observation

To filter my feelings about starness

Abstract Conceptualization

To study the science of stars

Active Experimentation

To steer by a star . . . finding uses of stars in my life

Different Learners, Different Gifts

As educators, we must recognize that many different kinds of talents go into any successful venture. We must begin to apply equal value to those differences. Let the Imaginative, Analytic, Common Sense and Dynamic Learners refine and share their gifts. By valuing them all, they will begin to develop the skills that *do not* come to them naturally, without guilt or defensiveness. They will become the best of who they are.

We need to design methods of learning that allow our students:

1. to develop their own natural gifts,

2. to understand and appreciate the natural gifts of others,

3. to go "around the circle" in a spiral form of increasing complexity, granting each the opportunity to refine her/his best style while experiencing and developing alternative styles.

We just have to look around to see people in need of all sorts of skills. Take one example, that of a manufacturing enterprise. The personnel manager deals with the most concrete phenomena of all, human beings. Personnel managers tend to fall into the first quadrant. They take in information concretely and they process it reflectively. They are watchers, observers. They trust their sense/feeling judgments. The One Learners are highly skilled with people. But they must also have highly developed abstract abilities, because they need to apply the abstract (generalities) to the concrete (individuals).

While they possess the gifts of the One Learners, they also must "go around the circle" to function successfully. The center of their focus is the concrete and the reflective, but in order to be successful they must develop the ability to apply the abstract (generalities) to the concrete (individuals). And of course, they must also make decisions, so they need to be active as well as reflective. They use their natural gifts as Type One Learners, but they also need to develop the skills of the other learning quadrants.

A research and design expert in the same firm deals primarily with the abstract and the reflective, the gifts of the Type Two Learner. S/he formulates ideas into concepts and prepares designs for engineering. The research and design expert, however, cannot afford to ignore the demands of the market, the concrete consumers, but the focus is the abstract and the reflective.

The engineer takes the abstract and processes it by doing it. S/he takes a design and builds it. S/he is a thinker-doer, the qualities of the Type Three Learners. The majority of engineers fall into the third quadrant. That is why hands-on experiences are so vital for the Type Three Learner, Kolb has

stated that these people prefer to deal only with things they can locate in time and space. Yet they are grossly mismanaged in our schools. Hands-on experiences, through which they learn best, exist mainly in vocational programs. But an aspiring engineer must succeed in college preparatory classes where hands-on experiences are virtually nonexistent.

And finally, the marketing person deals with the concrete, and does so by doing it, by trying it, the skills of the Type Four Learner. A salesperson needs to understand what is happening "on the street." There is no question of this, the job demands it. To be successful a salesperson must also understand how the product is made, and how it works. In addition s/he must have highly developed people skills, as in the case of the personnel manager. But the focus of the Type Four Learner is the combination of concrete and active.

Each of us deals with the concrete and the abstract in varying degrees and from different angles. Each of us deals with the active and reflective processing dimensions in varying degrees and from different angles. People are attracted to different kinds of employment and different disciplines of study based on the structure of those disciplines and the type of work they enjoy.

So the ladder model by itself is inadequate, for it implies that people with natural penchants for the concrete are less intelligent than those with natural penchants for the abstract, and in addition ignores the processing dimension of active and reflective.

Our students are different. They approach learning from different centers of focus. We must teach to all of them.

Part Two

Right and Left
Brain Processing

Chapter Five

CONTESTANT #1   CONTESTANT #2

Intellect
vs.
Intuition

ROUND ONE

DEFINITIONS:

Intellect: COLLECTION OF LEARNED FACTS. NO GUARANTEE OF RELEVANCY.

Intuition: INSPIRATION AND PERCEPTION SPRINGING FROM UNLIMITED RESERVOIR OF INNER TRUTH.

Intellect: DON'T CROSS. EACH YEAR THOUSANDS DIE IN TRAFFIC ACCIDENTS.

Intuition: DANGER!

Intellect: DIFFERENT SUBTLE HUES COMBINED INTO A HARMONIOUS MASS.

Intuition: PRETTY!

Intellect: CHARACTER DISORDER RESULTING IN CHRONIC IRRITABILITY.

Intuition: DUCK!

ZAP!

SCORE

Intellect ⦋0⦌   Intuition ⦋1⦌

RUSSELL MYERS

Two Kinds Of Brain Processing

Research on right and left brain functions began with Dr. Roger Sperry[1] during the 1950s. Dr. Sperry conducted a series of animal studies in which the corpus callosum, a thick nerve cable composed of nerve fibers that cross-connect the two cerebral hemispheres, was severed.

This connector is composed of 200 million fibers and provides a rapid pathway for memory and learning between the two hemispheres. The function of the corpus callosum, the largest collection of nerve fibers in the human body at one location, was an enigma during the 19th century. Dr. Sperry split the brains of monkeys and cats, completely severing the connections. The results were amazing. There was no great change in behavior. Their habits, gaits, and co-ordination remained unchanged following this drastic surgery. But when the animals were trained to specific tasks, they were found to have two independent minds, each with its own recognition, memory, and decision system.

In the 1960s, similar operations were performed on a limited number of human patients. These patients were individuals suffering from intractable epilepsy, patients whose seizures were spreading through the corpus callosum, from one hemisphere to the other, as many as forty times a day. All chemical measures had been tried to no avail. Neurosurgeons Phillip Vogel and Joseph Bogen consulted with Sperry in the hope that by severing the corpus callosum the attacks could be limited to one hemisphere. After much consultation, the first "split-brain" operation was performed on a human. As a result, the attacks were controlled. They were fewer in number, and the patient exhibited no outward disabilities.

A series of subtle and ingenious tests were then devised by Sperry and his associates to find out what was now going on in the two separated hemispheres. And, as in the cats and monkeys, two separate minds could be demonstrated.

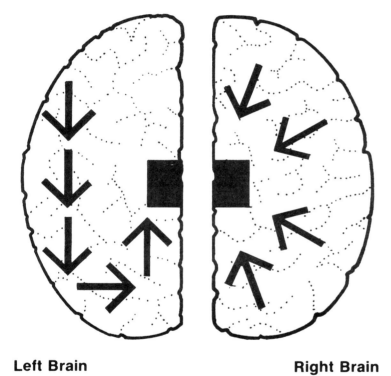

Left Brain   **Right Brain**

The major findings were:

1. *The two halves of the brain, right and left hemispheres, process information differently.*

It had long been known that the *functions* of the two hemispheres were different. Speech resides in the left brain and spatial capability in the right. But what was not known was that in *processing* information and stimuli, the left brain does a *lineal* type of processing, a sequential type, while the right brain uses a *global* process in which data is perceived, absorbed, and processed even while it is in the process of changing.

As Bogen stated, these differences in how the two brains process information are the most significant differences between the left and right hemispheres.[2]

The two hemispheres process information differently.

Equally important was the finding that:

2. *In the split-brain patient, there seem to be two different people up there, each with his/her favorite ways of processing information, each with a different mode of thinking.*

We are a two-brained species, each having its special mind.

That means that "rather than being a half-brained species, we are a two-brained species, each having its special mind."[3] We who have an intact corpus callosum preserve our sense of being a unified person by the melding of the two different kinds of perception. Experiments with split-brain patients have shown "the qualitative differences in the methods used to achieve comprehension are profound, and even greater than could have been predicted."[4]

What we educators need to do is to develop teaching methodologies which will effectively teach to *both* modes. The brain dominance researchers have pointed the way. As Sperry put it, "There appear to be two modes of thinking, verbal and non-verbal, represented rather separately in left and right hemispheres...our educational system, as well as science in general, tends to neglect the nonverbal form of intellect. What is comes down to is that modern society discriminates against the right hemishpere."[5]

Concurring, Bogen wrote, "Learning of almost any idea is likely to be better if both methods are used. We are accustomed to hear of the culturally disadvantaged....those persons whose (left mode) potential has remained underdeveloped for lack of relevant exposure. There is likely a lack of (right mode) development is persons whose only education consists of the three R's."[6]

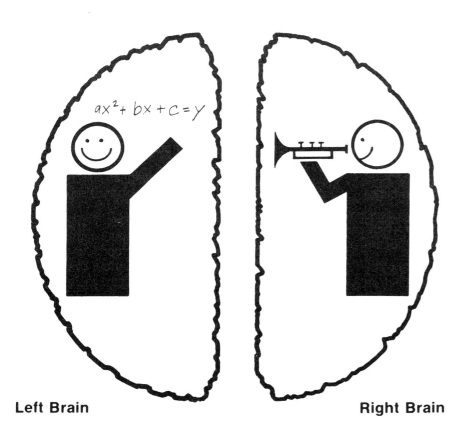

$$ax^2 + bx + c = y$$

Left Brain

Right Brain

The third finding from the split-brain research was:

3. *Both hemispheres are equally important.*

During the 19th century, it was believed the left hemisphere was superior due to the location of speech. Because language capability is of overwhelming importance in our culture, the language function has been emphasized most of the time.

This third finding, that the two modes are of equal importance, was not considered valid in the past because the left brain, the "good" brain, was doing this obviously human thing...using symbols to describe the past, predict the future, communicate . . . all the things that animals cannot do. Almost as though the right brain were some kind of spare tire.[7]

The two modes are of equal importance.

The left and right hemispheres
of the brain
process information
and experience differently.

The left does verbal things.
The left likes sequence.
The left sees the trees.
The left likes structure.

Left brains love school.

The right does visual-spatial things.
The right likes random patterns.
The right sees the forest.
The right is fluid and spontaneous.

Right brains hang around school
and hope they catch on.

School teaches us
not to trust our right mode of knowing;
so our subsequent use of it
makes us feel guilty,
less rational,
less intelligent.

Whereas the reality is
our virtually exclusive emphasis
on the left mode
makes us "stiff with technique
far from the scanning eye,"[8]
constrained to miss the mystery.

It's not that our right mode
stops functioning in school;
it's just that our ability to hear it,
to respond to it, to believe in it,
suffers terrible neglect.

The right mode sees relationships.
It grabs for the whole.
It draws the big circle.
It goes after the significant idea,
the ideas that connect.

(Content is relatively easy to master
once it has been given
a conceptual framework,
a connection that makes meaning.)

While the left mode
recognizes the relation
of the new
to the old,
the right mode
explores all the new material.

Together they move toward wholeness.

Knowledge is not fragmented.
Knowledge is coherent and whole.

How well we remember
the things we learn
depends on how well engaged
both hemishperes were
when we first learned it.

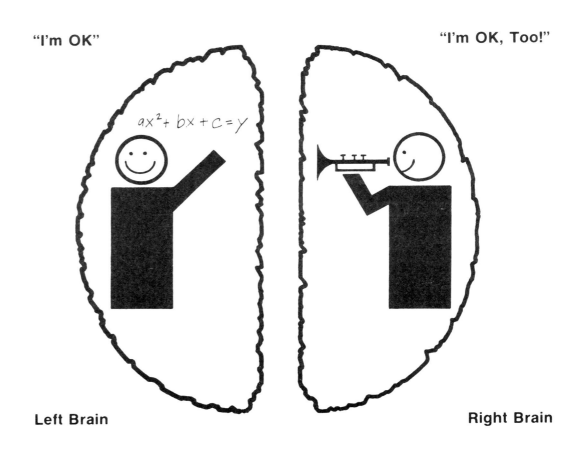

The Concept of Hemisphericity:
"*An individual is held to rely more on one mode of processing than another.*"[9]
Joseph Bogen

People who approach learning
with a left-mode processing preference
have beautiful gifts.
They are systematic,
they solve problems by looking at the parts,
they are sequential and are excellent planners.
They are analytic.

People who approach learning
with a right-mode processing preference
have beautiful gifts.
They see patterns,
they solve problems by looking at
the whole picture.
They are random and arrive
at accurate conclusions
in the absence of logical justification.
They are intuitive.

People who are wholebrained have both sets of beautiful gifts.

People who access their whole brain
flex and flow.
They have both sets of beautiful gifts.

The goal of education
should be
to help our students
develop the flexible use
of their whole brain.

If our schools lavish attention
on left-mode learning,
learners who favor the left mode
must do very well.
How wonderful for left-mode learners,
how sad for right-mode learners.

The dichotomy between the two
modes of knowing
has gone on long enough.
It is a false dichotomy.
It is time to teach
both analysis and synthesis.
It is time to teach
to the whole brain,
intellectual and intuitive,
mind and heart,
content centered and student centered.

We should encourage greater right-mode participation in the process of education.

We need to lecture and interact,
to show them how and to let them try it,
to have them memorize
and learn to question the experts,
to give answers and ask better questions,
to train their minds
while valuing the responses from their hearts,
to solve problems and to find problems,
to exercise the intellect and the imagination,
to hold on to our best traditional techniques
and to add new ones,
to teach them the best that civilization offers
and give them the courage to improve it.

Research shows
our teaching must change
if we are to maximize growth.

Our goal is the fusion
of analysis and intuition:
to set up environments
where guessing and divergent thinking
are encouraged,
coupled with the rigor of theoretical
excellence.

We need the time-oriented
vertical thinking of the left mode
and the timeless lateral thinking
of the right.

Right and left must work together.

Of course, truly teaching the whole brain would require whole new categories of learning. This report card of the future, published by the *Brain/Mind Bulletin,* is not so fanciful.[10]

GRADE	SCHOOL *DaVinci Elementary*
SEMESTER ENDING June	PRINCIPAL *R. B. Fuller*

	Mid-Semester Mark
SPATIAL RELATIONSHIPS	B
INTUITION	B
INSIGHT	C
GENERATES IDEAS FREELY	C
DAYDREAMING/REVERIE	C
GESTALT PERCEPTION	B+
ESTHETIC SENSIBILITY:	
Color	C+
Form	C
Music	B-
Poetry	D

Teacher's comments:

School psychologist suggests remedial imagination.

Explanation of marks:

A-Outstanding **B**-Very Good **C**-Satisfactory
D-Needs Improvement **F**-Unsatisfactory

WORK HABITS

Able to transcend space/time limitations	C
Is flexible	C-
Listens attentively — with third ear	C
Follows directions unless better idea occurs	B
Completes assignments — when useful	A-
Makes good use of time: Fantasizing	D
Creating	D
Meditating	C

CITIZENSHIP

Accepts responsibility	A
Respects authority — if there is justification for respect	B
Respects rights and property of others	B
Shows empathy/telepathy	B

Teacher's signature *C. Bronte*

Parent's signature _____

Some Right- and Left-Mode Characteristics

This list is presented in the hope that it may help generate ideas for variations on teaching strategies.

Left Mode

Rational
Responds to verbal instructions
Controlled, systematic experiments
Problem solves by logically and sequentially looking at the parts of things
Objective
Looks at differences
Is planned and structured
Prefers established, certain information
Analyzes
Primary reliance on language in thinking and remembering
Prefers talking and writing
Prefers objective tests
Controls feelings
Responsive to structure
Prefers hierarchical authority
Talks, and talks and talks
Sees cause and effect
Is theoretical
More sensitive to verbal sounds
Engaged by subtle conventions in grammatical sequencing
Excels in propositional language
Sees design details
Localized and discretely organized
Digitalized
Formal laws
Superior in:
Writing
Digit and letter recognition
Nameable shapes
Word recognition and recall
Phonics discriminations
Slower, serial, analytic difference detection
Draws on previously accumulated, organized information

Right Mode

Intuitive
Responds to demonstrated instructions
Open-ended, random experiments
Problem solves by hunching, looking for patterns and configurations
Subjective
Looks at similarities
Is fluid and spontaneous
Prefers elusive, uncertain information
Synthesizes
Primary reliance on images in thinking and remembering
Prefers drawing and manipulating
Prefers essay tests
Free with feelings
Responsive to ambiance
Prefers collegial authority
Is mute, uses pictures, not words
Sees correspondences
Is experiential
More sensitive to natural sounds, i.e., water running
Engaged by patterns of sound that have naturalistic meaning
Excels in poetic, metaphoric language
Sees overall design form
Diffuse organization
Patterned
Paradigms--shared theories
Superior in:
Drawing
Verbal material when imagery is used to code
Nonverbal dimensions: light, hue, depth perception
Photographs, schematic figures
Tactile discriminations
Rapid, global, identity matching
Draws on unbounded qualitative patterns that are not sequential, but cluster around felt images

Some Right-Mode Techniques

Here is a partial list of activities we believe favor the right mode.

Patterning
Metaphors
Mind-mapping
Visualization
Imagery
All forms of poetry
All Fine Arts
Modalities: Auditory, Visual, Kinesthetic
Mixed modalities
Analogies
The use of paradox
Connections of all kinds
Most forms of doing
Building
Role-playing
Creative dramatics
Creative writing
Clustering
Movement
Dance
All synthesis
Geometry (probably all mathematical conceptualizing)
Spatial relationships of all kinds
Demonstrations
Experiments
Configurations
All activities in which intuition is honored

Chapter Six

**DISTRIBUTION OF LEARNING STYLES:
HOW MANY TEACHERS AND
ADMINISTRATORS
ARE TYPE ONES, TWOS, THREES, AND
FOURS?**

In order to determine what relationship exists between learning styles and right-, left- and whole-brain processing preferences, I administered the Kolb Learning Style Inventory[1] and the McCarthy Hemispheric Mode Indicator[2] to 2,367 teachers and administrators during 1986-87.

The following tables show the results of these surveys. The sample includes all grade levels of teaching, pre-school to post secondary, and all the content areas, as well as self-contained classroom teachers and special education teachers.

The participants are from all regions of the United States, including Hawaii, as well as a sizeable representation of Canadians.

The numbers of participants vary in each of the tables presented because some of the teachers and administrators did not answer all the question we asked.

In Table I, Type Two Learners are the highest number followed closely by Type Fours.

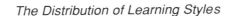

The Distribution of Learning Styles

N=2,367

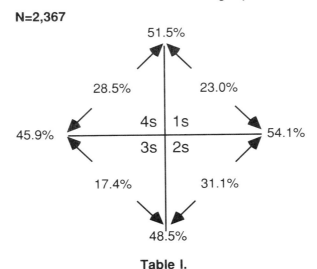

Table I.

Type Ones comprise about one-fourth of the group and Type Threes are the smallest number. The Type Three Learners consistently are the least represented in all of the teaching staffs we have surveyed. My speculation is that their pragmatic nature, their insistence that school be relevant, drives them away.

When we add the number of participants from Quadrants One and Four together, we can see the numbers of teachers who tend toward the concrete end of the perception dimension. 51.5% of the sample favor the concrete.

When we contrast this number with the sum of the participants from Quadrants Two and Three, we see that 48.5% favor the abstract end of the perceiving dimension. Although slightly tipped in favor of the concrete, these results seem to indicate a fair balance between concrete and abstract preferences in perceiving.

In order to look at the balance or lack of balance along the processing dimension from watching (Reflective Observation) to doing (Active Experimentation), we first add the number of participants in Quadrants One and Two and see a reflective penchant of 54.1%. We contrast that with the sum of participants who were found in Quadrants Three and Four. The results show the reflective dimension has a 10% edge over the active dimension. Given the emphasis in our schools on quiet reading and the passive intake of facts, it is lovely to see such balance between reflection and action.

LEARNING STYLES AND GENDER: A SIGNIFICANT RELATIONSHIP

The balance among the four Learning Styles shifts dramatically when we divide the group into female and male.

There are more Type One and Type Four females than males. 25% of the women are Type Ones, and 32.7% of the women are Type Four. So the total of females who prefer the sensing/feeling dimension of perceiving is 57.7%.

The percentage of women who prefer the abstract dimension of perceiving is 42.2%.

In contrast there are more Type Two and Type Three males than females. 61% of the men are either Type Two or Type Three Learners. So the number of males who prefer the abstract dimension of perceiving, the thinkers, is considerably higher than the men who prefer the concrete dimension, the feelers, 39%.

Is this a reflection of a societal bias affecting the freedom of men to feel and women to abstract? I have felt for some time that it is easier for women to maintain a balance between feeling and thinking than it is for men. Perhaps these figures are an indication of that.

I believe the Kolb LSI shows the bias operating against the feeling approach to learning for men. But more seriously, I believe it underlines a deep-seated bias against all feeling in education.

There are differences between men and women on the processing dimensions as well, the reflective versus the active characteristics.

When the percentages of women in Quadrants One and Two, the reflective processing quadrants, are added together, 52.5% of the women report a preference for the reflective approach to processing experience and information.

When the percentages of women in Quadrants Three and Four, the doing dimension, are added together, we find that 47.5% of the women in this sample prefer the active dimension.

The male percentages show a greater difference on the processing dimension. 56.9% are reflective, and 43.1% prefer active processing.

While both groups indicate higher scores for the reflective dimension, there is less difference in the women, 5%, than the men at l3%.

Perhaps this preference for reflection in both sexes is a result of the unfortunate but ubiquitous penchant in our schools for the passive intake of information as the primary method for acquiring knowledge.

Learning Styles and Gender

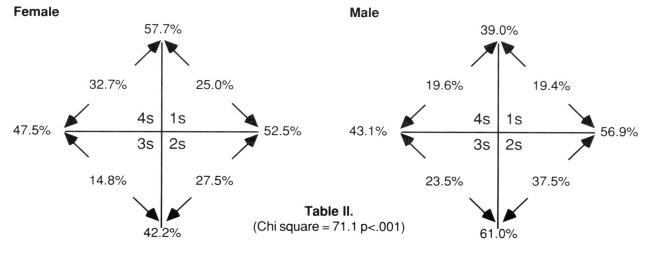

Table II.
(Chi square = 71.1 p<.001)

THE HEMISPHERIC MODE PREFERENCES OF TEACHERS: RIGHT OR LEFT MODE?

The McCarthy Hemispheric Mode Indicator was used to determine the brain mode preferences of the same sample of teachers and administrators.

The instrument measures preferences in the way individuals approach learning with a bias for right- or left-mode processing techniques.

The test also measures tendencies for wholebrain approaches. Wholebrainedness seems to be a preference for approaching learning experiences and opportunities with a flexibility and fluency for both types of processing strategies.

As Table III indicates, right-mode teachers make up a third of the sample, the left-mode teachers 40%.

When we add wholebrain favoring percentages to mode percentages,
we see a 43.1% right-mode preference,
and a 49.2% left-mode preference.

Again the balance is heartening. It is interesting as well. If I am right in my contention that the educational system is strongly biased in favor of left-mode structures and teaching methods, it is a credit to our teachers that their numbers reflect such a balance.

While this finding is hopeful in terms of a healthy diversity in our teaching and administrative staffs, it also causes some concern. Why do our teaching methods remain so solidly left mode if half of our teachers favor either wholebrain or right-mode approaches to learning?

I believe the answer is that the structure overwhelms the practice. The left-mode characteristics which are so prevalent place emphasis on correct and right information, rewards for conformity, the stages of development, compartmentalized content, etc. The structure of the educational enterprise mitigates against right-mode, ergo wholebrain approaches to learning.

This is a primary change we must seek if we are to honor the students who come to us with a bias for approaching learning from the right mode and if we are to teach all our students to be excellent.

N=1,813
WHOLE SAMPLE

40%	9.2%	7.8%	9.7%	33.4%
LEFT	WHOLEBRAIN FAVORING LEFT	WHOLEBRAIN	WHOLEBRAIN FAVORING RIGHT	RIGHT

TABLE III

HEMISPHERIC MODE PREFERENCES
OF FEMALES AND MALES:
A SIGNIFICANT RELATIONSHIP

In hemispheric mode preferences,
again women come up more balanced as a group
with 48.2% favoring the Right Mode
and 44.0% favoring the Left Mode.

Men reflect a definite preference for
the Left Mode at 58.6%
over the Right Mode at 33.5%.

This is not surprising as we now have a clearly
established relationship between the four
learning styles and right- and left-mode
processing.

The right mode is related to concrete experience
(Learning Styles One and Four) and the left mode
to abstract conceptualization (Learning Styles
Two and Three).

FEMALES: N=1,243

35.1%	8.9%	7.8%	10.5%	37.7%
LEFT	WHOLEBRAIN FAVORING LEFT	WHOLEBRAIN	WHOLEBRAIN FAVORING RIGHT	RIGHT

LEFT PLUS WHOLEBRAIN LEFT
= 44%

RIGHT PLUS WHOLEBRAIN RIGHT
= 48.2%

MALES: N=570

49.3%	9.3%	7.9%	7.5%	26.0%
LEFT	WHOLEBRAIN FAVORING LEFT	WHOLEBRAIN	WHOLEBRAIN FAVORING RIGHT	RIGHT

LEFT PLUS WHOLEBRAIN LEFT
=58.6%

RIGHT PLUS WHOLEBRAIN RIGHT
= 33.5%

TABLE IV
(Chi square = 39.4 p<.001)

LEARNING STYLES AND HEMISPHERIC DOMINANCE: A SIGNIFICANT RELATIONSHIP

N=1,886

	ONES	TWOS	THREES	FOURS
Learning Style Totals	23.4%	30.8%	17.5%	28.2%
Right	44.8%	9.2%	14.2%	62.0%
Wholebrain favoring right	14.4%	5.5%	5.8%	12.6%
Wholebrain	12.6%	5.5%	7.0%	6.8%
Wholebrain favoring left	9.5%	11.0%	11.5%	5.6%
Left	18.7%	68.8%	61.5%	13.0%

TABLE V
(Chi square = 653.1 p<.001)

There is a strong tendency toward left mode in Quadrants Two and Three and a strong tendency toward right mode in Quadrants One and Four. So the relationship between the concrete and the right mode and the abstract and the left mode is a strong one. Schools primarily teach at the bottom of the 4MAT circle, Left Mode, Quadrant Two and Left Mode, Quadrant Three, giving information to passive receivers and requiring the completion of workbooks and questions at the ends of chapters in order to get to the next chapter.

I call this the pendulum style of teaching, back and forth across the bottom of the circle, rather than the completeness of all four quadrants progressing from

experience
 to reflection
  to conceptualization
   to experimentation,

using both modes of information processing, right and left, in a movement

from "in here" to "out there," from subjective to objective, from synthesis to analysis and back again.

So that our students may go through the complete cycle.

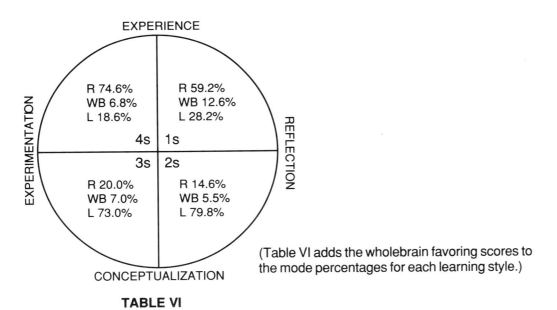

(Table VI adds the wholebrain favoring scores to the mode percentages for each learning style.)

TABLE VI

The importance of this information is to convince educators of the need to focus on both right and left mode techniques of instruction even while we struggle to understand what they are.

How do we deal with the right mode, with its gestalt, intuitive hold on reality? Bogen calls it the appositional mind. Webster defines **apposition** as the placing of things in juxtaposition (grammar), also as the deposition of successive layers upon those already present (biology), or the definition of the appositional eye: an insect eye in which entering light reaches the retina of each segment as a single spot and the image is a composite of all the spots.

The percentages on the HMI indicate there are right, left, and wholebrain learners in each of the four learning style quadrants. So the decision to create a teaching model where left and right mode techniques are alternated through a four learning style cycle seems to be a common sense approach to teaching.

Learning Styles and Career Choice

Kolb has tested the relationship between individual learning styles and the types of careers people choose. He reports that undergraduate business majors tend to have learning styles consistent with the fourth quadrant characteristics, while engineers often fall in the third quadrant. History, English, political science and psychology majors have first quadrant learning styles, while mathematics, chemistry, economics and sociology majors have quadrant two learning styles. Physics majors are very abstract, falling between the second and third quadrants.

"Elementary education majors and teachers are characterized by a high concrete experience orientation. Interest in working with children may be associated with a concrete orientation. Alcoholism counselors/therapists and human services workers also show a very high concrete experience orientation, along with very high reflective observation scores, the first quadrant characteristics of people-oriented professions. Organizational development specialists have a similar but less pronounced pattern, particularly on the active to reflective scale. Medical school groups show an interesting change from the first to fourth years. In the first year, they are the highest scoring sample on abstract conceptualization, probably because of the abstract nature of medical school selection procedures. In the fourth year group, however, this changes markedly toward active experimentation. Industrial salesmen have the highest
score of any group on active experimentation (the doing dimension) and computer programmers show the high abstract orientation one would predict for a very symbol-oriented job. The patterns of scores taken collectively across all the different groups suggest that learning style scores show sufficient variability across different populations to be useful in assessing the learning styles that characterize occupations and groups."[3]

Kolb believes that this data show a person's "undergraduate education is a major factor in the development of his/her learning style. Whether this is because individuals are shaped by the fields they enter or because of selection processes that put people into and out of disciplines is an open question at this point. Most probably both factors are operating. People choose fields which are consistent with their learning styles and are further shaped to fit the learning norms of their field once they are in it. When there is a mismatch between the field's learning norms and the individual's learning style, people will either change or leave the field."[4]

Kolb has also found "strong correlations between the learning style of students and their ratings of the learning style of the teacher 'who has influenced them most.' These correlations show a strong similarity between the student's learning style and that of the teacher who influenced him/her."

This bring us to the additional question of what causes what. Do charismatic teachers cause their students to adapt to their teaching styles, or do these teachers adapt themselves to their students' learning styles?

Teaching Styles or Learning Styles or Both?

Kolb has stated that people choose fields based on congruence between their learning styles and the norms of those fields. I believe Kolb is right. However, does a "special" teacher, special to that particular student, project such a high value for one method of learning that the valued method remains with that student throughout a lifetime? Does the natural penchant for learning return after that teacher's influence is but a memory? I do not believe any of us can answer that question. Whether a spark was fired that flamed an existing potential or whether such students actually "switch gears" remains an enigma. Human beings are too complex for anyone to speak with certainty about such phenomena.

For this very reason, I find it essential that all four modes of learning be taught to all students and, most importantly, *equally valued.* This is necessary not only to allow the natural progression "around the circle" so vital for integrative education but also to allow students to choose their most comfortable places, their own best learning styles. I am often asked to assist teachers in "matching" teaching styles with student learning styles. I am always hesitant. First I do not believe one learning style, however carefully refined, is sufficient without understanding its weaknesses as well as its strengths. My firm conviction, already stated many times in this book, is that students need to progress through the entire learning cycle in order to develop the skills that do not come naturally, while refining their own innate gifts. Secondly, any "matching" operation in a school necessitates labels, and we already have too many labels in education now.

Do we need more?

Many people in my audiences ask for *the test,* the test that will enable them to identify both the learning styles of their students as well as their brain dominance patterns.

I value the research of David Kolb as well as my own work with The Hemispheric Mode Indicator. However, I always remind my survey takers that the results of the battery indicate their learning styles and brain dominance *according to Kolb and McCarthy.* The individual is the only true judge of how valuable the instruments may be.

So when I am requested to supply *the test,* I ask why. Are people planning to separate their students into groups and teach them in only one of four modes? Won't the future life experiences of their students present them with many types of learning situations? Can students really afford to neglect the other three dimensions of the learning cycle? Is the purpose in wanting to discover the dominant brain modality of their students to teach right mode students with only right mode techniques and left mode students with only left mode techniques? What of the goal of integration, developing alternative skills and modes of learning while refining innate gifts?

Betty Edwards speaks eloquently of the need for students to experience the "shift" from left to right mode functioning and from right to left mode functioning, in order that they may learn to use both types of brain processing to enhance their potential.

"I really feel that to teach to a person's dominant mode may not in fact turn out to be exactly the best thing to do. If that dominant mode happens to be dominant left hemisphere, their non-use of the opposite mode may in the long run be more destructive. The identification of learning styles may be a lead in understanding how not to beam all the information at the verbal left brain simply because that is where the child does best, but instead to teach that child, first of all, about his or her own brain and to help the child to use the other half as well. . . We need to pay more attention to developing strategies that will encompass that great complexity of individual differences. I think that is the better way to go rather than trying to define all the differences."[5]

I recall one superintendent who requested my "kit." I told him I had no kit and asked what he would do with his students if indeed such an entity existed. Using the Common Sense Learners as an example, those who need hands-on-experiences, he told me he would place them together in one class and require them "to do projects and watch films." This would be a distorted use of the instruments. First of all, the instruments available are only tools. As we all know, there are so many variables in taking a test, that we should be very hesitant to use tests to classify students rigidly. Secondly, as you will see in Chapter Seven (the complete model), students, if given choices, will reveal their best learning styles through those choices. But their choices only reveal their most comfortable learning penchants at *that* place, at *that* time in *their* level of development and in some particular situation. And thirdly, we should not deny students the benefits of learning from each other, experiencing the learning styles of other students, as well as providing them with the opportunity to experience shifts in brain functioning.

Assume we could determine accurately the brain dominance of particular students as strongly right: a concrete, intuitive, gestalt, nonsequential penchant in approaching learning. I grant that such students need the opportunity to experience learning through the medium of their own natural gifts, where teachers allow them to "shine" in their own inimitable way, their most comfortable style. However, they also need (and to no small degree) to develop the abilities to abstract, to intellectualize, to break down and classify and to use sequential logic. To do less for such students is to deny their potential.

We can use the available instruments as tools. We can identify strength and weaknesses with the reservations I have stated. But foremost in our search for answering individual differences in students must be in finding strategies that encompass the great wonderful complexity we serve. That is where the emphasis should be. Rather than defining the differences, let us allow our students to develop naturally, giving all differences equal value.

Learning styles encompass so many variables, so much diversity, that we cannot ever assume that tests fully measure them.

Learning styles are:

Characteristic penchants for
perceiving and processing
information and experience
that are unique to individuals
and developmental through life stages.
They are comprised of complex interactions of
physiological,
psychological,
environmental
and situational variables.

The key words tell us more about learning styles.

penchants
particular preferences that are predictive
in terms of response to instruction,
what we do first.

for perceiving and processing
diverse assortment of characteristics
having to do with
the *method* by which individuals approach
and process experience.

experience and information
everything that happens to us, everything we see,
hear, touch, feel, taste, smell and sense.

that are unique to individuals
as unique as physiognomy, body height and weight, color of
hair, eyes, bone structure, etc.

and developmental through life stages
Kolb has found people become more reflective as they pass through mid-life. Surely any period of change in our lives
influences our approach to experience.

comprised of complex interactions of

physiological
handedness as related to brain dominance
sex differences
neurophysiological differences
penchants for modalities.[6]

psychological
ego strength
level of family rigidity
sex models in the family
basic optimism and sense of humor
parental love and support
consistency in the family
(entire emotional atmosphere of the home and the learning institution)

environmental
cultural differences, i.e., definition of highest levels of thinking
held by a particular culture[7]
societal values as to male and female

situational
pressures to succeed in only certain ways
empathy and skill of teachers
philosophy of learning in a particular teaching institution
and financial resources.

Much research remains to be done on all of these variables. However, we now know these differences exist. We must begin to capitalize on them. We must begin to teach to all our students.

Part Three

The Complete Model

Chapter Seven

Major Premises:

1
- Human beings *perceive* experience and information in different ways.
- Human beings *process* experience and information in different ways.
- The combinations formed by our own perceiving and processing techniques form our unique learning styles.

2
- There are four major identifiable learning styles.
- They are all equally valuable.
- Students need to be comfortable about their own unique learning style.

3
- Type One Learners are primarily interested in personal meaning. Teachers need to *Create a Reason.*
- Type Two Learners are primarily interested in the facts as they lead to conceptual understanding. Teachers need to *Give Them the Facts* that deepen understanding.
- Type Three Learners are primarily interested in how things work. Teachers need to *Let Them Try It.*
- Type Four Learners are primarily interested in self discovery. Teachers need to *Let Them Teach It to Themselves and to Others.*

4
- All students need to be taught in all four ways, in order to be comfortable and successful part of the time while being stretched to develop other learning abilities.
- All students will "shine" at different places in the learning cycle, so they will learn from each other.

5
- The 4MAT System moves through the learning cycle *in sequence,* teaching in all four modes and incorporating the four combinations of characteristics.
- The sequence is a natural learning progression.

6
- Each of the four learning styles needs to be taught with both right- and left-mode processing techniques.
- The right-mode dominant students will be comfortable half of the time and will learn to adapt the other half of the time.
- The left-mode dominant students will be comfortable half of the time and will learn to adapt the other half of the time.

7
- The development and integration of all four styles of learning and the development and integration of both right- and left-mode processing skills should be a major goal of education.

8
- Students will come to accept their strengths and learn to capitalize on them, while developing a healthy respect for the uniqueness of others, and furthering their ability to learn in alternative modes without the pressure of "being wrong."

9
- The more comfortable they are about who they are, the more freely they learn from others.

Teaching to All Four Learning Styles
Using Right- and Left-Mode Techniques

Remember
each of the four learning style types
has a quadrant, or place,
where s/he is most comfortable,
where success comes easily.

The Imaginative Learners, those who fall in
quadrant one,
prefer to learn through a combination of
sensing/feeling and watching.

The Analytic Learners, those who fall in
quadrant two,
prefer to learn through a combination of
watching and thinking through concepts.

The Common Sense Learners, those who fall in
quadrant three,
prefer to learn by thinking through concepts
and trying things out for themselves,
by doing.

The Dynamic Learners, those who fall in
quadrant four,
prefer to learn by doing and sensing/feeling.

The 4Mat System is designed so all four types
of learners
are comfortable
some of the time.

This chapter will explain in depth each
progressive phase of instruction
as teachers move through all four quadrants,
as they go "around the circle."
It will also show how to use
right and left mode techniques
in each quadrant.

The role of the teacher changes as s/he goes
around the circle;
this chapter will illustrate those changes.
The skills to be taught change as you go
around the circle;
this chapter will explain the skills to be taught
in each quadrant.

A sample lesson plan will be used to help the
reader see the application
of these concepts. Part Four, which follows this
chapter, consists of
fifteen sample lesson plans, written by teachers
who are successfully using the model:

four designed for primary students,
four for intermediate,
three for middle school, and
four for high school.

The Learning Style Quadrants in Depth

The First Quadrant:
Integrating Experience with the Self

A process from **Concrete Experience to Reflective Observation.**
Sensing/Feeling to Watching/Reflecting.

All of the students go through all of the quadrants, but quadrant one appeals most to the Imaginative Learners. The favorite question of the Imaginative Learner is "Why?" You must create an environment or experience through which students can discover a reason. Hereafter, this co-creation of meaning by teacher and student is simply referred to as: Create a Reason.

The Type One Imaginative Learner's most comfortable place is the upper right corner of the model.

Concrete Experience

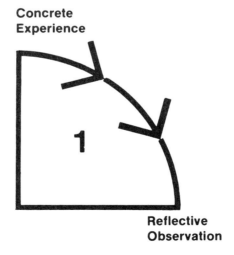

Reflective Observation

Teacher's Role = Motivator/Witness
Method = Simulation, Discussion

These types of learners rely heavily on personal experience and reflect on that experience. They absorb reality. These students are concerned with personal meaning. "Why do I need to learn this?" They check out their feelings and ideas through interaction with others. They function through synergy. Discussion and sharing are the means by which they "pull it all together." The teacher's role is motivator/witness.

Students need reasons to proceed with learning. All students do. But for the Imaginative Learners "Why?" is an absolute necessity. It seems simplistic to mention that students need reasons, but they are rarely given. Teachers assume students know that what is taught to them is necessary. Teachers assume *their* reasons are sufficient, that students will value what experts say they should learn. Not so. Students need reasons of their own.

Remember high school freshmen algebra? How many of us were given a reason to take algebra? We were taught a new inexplicable code. It was months before I realized how difficult my teacher had made the basics of algebra. I memorized the code. I solved for X and Y. But I never knew what X and Y were for. I believe that only students who have gone on to higher mathematics could tell us what algebra is for. Why algebra is not taught through concrete examples and meaningful applications is a question that has always perplexed me. Students could then understand what they are solving for.

If any students had the courage to ask, "Why algebra?" the answer would probably be one of the following:

"Because it is necessary for college."
"Because the study of algebra will train your mind."
"Because experts know high school students need to study algebra."
"Open your books!"

But to not answer such a question if to stifle motivation, smother it before it begins. And without motivation, quizzes and exams become games, ways to beat the system, rather than tools for students to check their progress. Such games are struggles between teachers and learners, where cheating flourishes.

What about poetry? Why did our pleasure in rhymes and musical sounds in the primary years turn to the groans of high school?

I remember the fun of jumping rope to

Old King Cole was a merry old soul,
A merry old soul was he.
He called for his pipe,
he called for his bowl,
he called for his fiddlers three.

and

Twinkle, twinkle little star, how I wonder who you are.
Up above the world so high, like a diamond in the sky.

Is it really such a big step from nursery rhymes to the wonders of haiku?

In the dark sky,
How they twinkle, how they shine.
All the little stars.

That poem was written by a small child enrolled in the Suzuki Talent Education Program. Here's another, written by a child in the same program:

Jonquils growing fast,
Getting taller every day
Spring is here at last.

The children who wrote these poems have reasons for enjoying poetry, their own real reasons, and their poems are expressions of their wonder. The world renowned violin teacher, Shinichi Suzuki, describes how he draws forth motivation in his young pupils (at three years of age) not only to express themselves in music but "to express all that is harmonious and best in human beings":

We encourage them to think of it as fun. Although we accept infants, at first we do not have them play the violin. First we teach the mother to play one piece so that she will be a good teacher at home. As for the child, we first have him simply listen at home to a record of the piece he will be learning... Until the parent can play one piece, the child does not play at all. This principle is very important indeed, because the parent may want him to do so, a three or four year-old child has no desire to learn the violin. The idea is to get the child to say, "I want to play too": so the first piece is played every day on the gramophone, and in the classroom he just watches the other children (and his mother) having their lessons. The proper environment is created for the child. The mother, moreover, both at home and in the classroom, plays on a small violin more suited to the child. The child will naturally before long take the violin away from his mother, thinking, "I want to play too." He knows the tune already. The other children are having fun, he wants to join in the fun. We have caused him to acquire this desire.[1]

Every teaching and training enterprise should begin by creating a desire. Even in adult education, where highly motivated students come for their own personal needs, teachers must give them reasons why the program is important. The teacher *must* take the time to discuss what s/he hopes to do and *why*. Giving them a reason, a need of their own for proceeding, is so simple and fundamental that one can only marvel that it is not done. Perhaps teachers who do not give reasons do not have reasons themselves. But it is inappropriate to lay the blame for this vacuum on teachers only.

In my teaching career, I have been interviewed many times for teaching positions. I was asked first for my credentials, next about my experience. In some rare instances, I was asked how I would teach my subject matter. But I have never been asked *why*. Not one administrator ever saw fit to ask me why my students might profit from what I was being hired to teach. A teacher who does not have a valid reason for teaching what s/he teaches, should simply not be teaching. I would think administrators would want to know this first.

I vividly recall a seminar I attended in Dallas. Various workshops were offered, and I chose one designed to "improve methods of instruction." The instructor asked us to sit in groups and handed us an algorithm, a step-by-step flow chart for making a frozen daiquiri. She told us our task was to teach a group of adults how to make this drink. She asked that we decide in our groups the first thing we would do. The other members of my group were all from the same company, one with an extensive training budget, including a posh facility for two week training sessions for all new employees. They decided, without any hesitation, that their first task would be to assemble all the necessary physical materials, and then they would take their trainees through the procedure step-by-step showing them how to do it. I interrupted and said, "First, I believe you should let them see and taste a frozen daiquiri, the finished product." They seemed surprised and asked why. I answered that I would need to know if my trainees either needed or wanted to learn how to make a frozen daiquiri before I would proceed.

I did not persuade them. When the instructor asked what our group had decided I had to file a minority report. That experience amazed me. Surely one would need to know whether or not the material was pertinent and why, in order to pass on that information and allow students to respond and discuss it. People do not learn because someone else wants them to. They learn because *they* want to.

Teachers as well as students need to understand the reasons for doing what they do. Without giving our students reasons and having reasons ourselves, all else fails. We must answer the question "Why?" or no real learning can occur. We must create a desire, a desire that is theirs, within them. That is the teacher's primary task.

So the 4Mat System is designed to begin by *creating a reason.* This is the focus of quadrant one, and the method is described below. It incorporates first a right mode technique to develop and refine right mode functioning and then moves to the second step of developing and refining the left mode. Both techniques incorporate the needs of the first quadrant Imaginative Learners, as well as initiating the study to be undertaken for the other three types of learners.

**Concrete Experience
(Sensing/Feeling)**

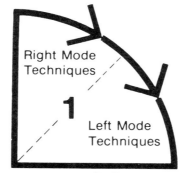

Right Mode
Techniques

1

Left Mode
Techniques

**Reflective Observation
(Watching/Reflecting)**

The skills that are addressed in Quadrant One include focusing skills and generating skills:

observing, questioning, visualizing, imagining, inferring, diverging,

as well as the group participation skills: brainstorming, listening, speaking and interacting.

The unit I have chosen to illustrate the use of the 4MAT System is for intermediate children, grades 4, 5, and 6. Its objectives are;

General: To increase enjoyment of poetry. (Affective)
To teach the skills of poetry analysis. (Cognitive)
To examine how people deal with defeat and failure. (Affective and Cognitive)

Specific: To read, understand, analyze, and enjoy "Casey at the Bat," by Ernest Lawrence Thayer (1863-1940).

**Concrete
Experience**

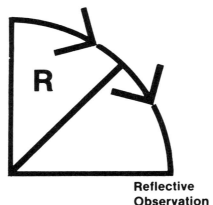

**Reflective
Observation**

Quadrant One: Integrating Experience with the Self

Step One

Create an Experience
Type One, Right Mode Learner most comfortable
Teacher Role — Motivator
Method — Discussion
Question to be answered — Why?
"Create a reason."

Divide children into groups of five.
Pass out "experience" sheets.

Experience Sheet:

Directions:
You will create a short skit to perform for the class.
One of you is the coach.
One of you is the star player.
One of you is the mother/father of the star player.
Two of you are excited, cheering fans.

It is the end of the game — basketball or baseball, whichever the group wishes. The star player has the entire game in his/her hands. Either two foul shots to win or last up at bat in the ninth inning with two outs, two people on base and the score 4 to 2. (The other team is winning.) The star player shoots and misses or strikes out.

Remember, everyone together in your group has to decide how each of you will act: facial expressions, body movements, words you will speak or cheers, boos, etc. You have ten minutes to plan your skit.

The rest of the period is spent watching the various skits.

Comments on Step One:

*Integrating Experience with the Self:
Creating an Experience*

In this step, the objective is to enter into the experience, to engage the self, and to integrate personal meaning with the experience. The children are allowed to interact with each other and with the main character in the poem, "Casey." They are encouraged to "be him." This is where they step *into* the material, where they experience it.

Allow them to decide what parts they will play. They can't all be Casey. Those students with a *concrete* orientation will love this exercise. Those with more *abstract* orientations will probably take lesser roles. That's fine. If children are shy, let them be shy. As they become more comfortable their shyness will lessen. Some people remain more shy than others all their lives. That is fine too. The introspective ones will get their chance to shine later in the process. And they will learn by watching each other. There are many forms "creating an experience" can take besides simulation. There are others listed in the lesson plans in Part Four.

The method here is interaction and discussion, the favorite method for the Type One Learners. The skills that are sharpened in this type of exercise are the skills at which Type One Learners excel: brainstorming, listening, speaking, interacting, and pulling together diverse elements.

Imagination and idea generation are encouraged, and these are characteristics of the Imaginative Learners. The right mode quality of this type of technique resides in the gestalt aspect of putting the skit together, and the entering into the experience rather than examining it from the outside. The right mode quality is in the concreteness of it, the need to "be it."

**Concrete
Experience**

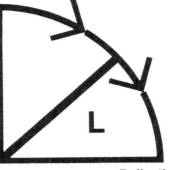

L

**Reflective
Observation**

Step Two

Reflecting on Experience

Type One, Left Mode Learner most comfortable.
Teacher Role — Witness
Method — Discussion
Question to be answered — Why?
"Create a reason."

Group discussion:

- How did you all feel for the star player?
- How do you think s/he felt?
- Is it understandable to feel that way when you lose, especially when everyone's counting on you?
- Do you think it's fair for everyone to count on one person to win?
- Do you sometimes feel the fans should come out and play and not just cheer and boo?
- How did your imagination work when you watched the skits?
- Were you filling in the details, imagining it was really happening?

Comments on Step Two:

Reflecting on Experience

The left mode aspect of reflecting on experience lies in the quality of analysis. Now the students examine the experience. The method is discussion, which is *the* method in the first quadrant, but the focus has changed. The students are now asked to step *outside* the experience and look at its parts.

Note: Teacher's role in this second step is to *witness* the personal value s/he sees and understands in poetry. This step is vital. This is leadership in teaching, to witness to the value of the material being presented.

I would wind up this discussion and end step two in the following way. I would give a little speech in which I would witness to the value of poetry. I would tell my students that images are formed by filling in the details. When we see a play on the stage, we imagine, we fill in the details. And when we read a poem, we see images in our minds, we fill in the details, we imagine. Sometimes we imagine so well, it's like we are there. That is when the poet has done a good job in writing a poem, when we see images and pictures in our minds. And when we feel what the poet felt and see what the poet saw.

I would tell them that is why I love poetry. It helps me to see and experience what someone else has seen and experienced. It helps me to stretch and grow and understand. Poetry builds bridges for us to cross. It helps us to grow. The poet is a bridge builder. I would end the class by reading the children the following poem for their enjoyment. And I would read it with care and feeling.

"The Bridge Builder"

An old man, going a lone highway,
Came at the evening, cold and grey,
To a chasm, vast and deep and wide,
Through which was flowing a sullen tide.
The old man crossed in the twilight dim —
That sullen stream had no fears for him;
But he turned, when he reached the other side,
And built a bridge to span the tide.

"Old man," said a fellow pilgrim near,
"You are wasting strength in building here.
Your journey will end with the ending day;
You never again must pass this way.
You have crossed the chasm, deep and wide,
Why build you the bridge at eventide?"

The builder lifted his old grey head.
"Good friend, in the path I have come," he said,
"There followeth after me today
A youth whose feet must pass this way.
This chasm that has been naught to me
To that fair-haired youth may a pitfall be.
He, too, must cross in the twilight dim;
Good friend, I am building the bridge for him."

Will Allen Dromgoole

The Second Quadrant:
Concept Formulation

A process of learning from **Reflective Observation to Abstract Conceptualization.**
Reflecting/Watching to Developing/Concepts.

All of the students go through this process, but quadrant two appeals most to the Analytic Learners.

The Type Two Learner's most comfortable place is the lower right corner of the model.

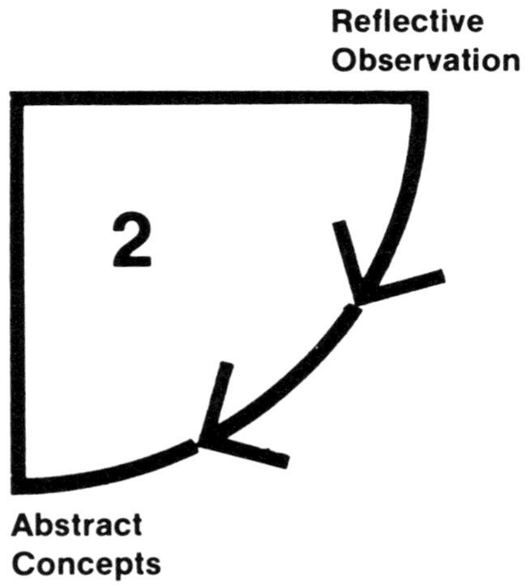

Reflective Observation

2

Abstract Concepts

Teacher's Role = "Teacher"

Method = Informational

The Analytic Learner is introspective and relies on intellectual ability as a primary focus for understanding. S/he forms reality. These students want to know "What?" They check out the experts. They want to know the facts. They want to know what the body of acknowledged knowledge is.

The teacher's role in quadrant two is "teacher" in the traditional sense of giving information. This is where the teacher's ability to organize material into priorities is crucial. What information, for example, is most important to analyze a poem? Most teachers do this well. That is what we are taught to do in our training. Giving information and organizing material is what administrators and parents expect us to do. Teach it to them and test them to see if they have "learned" it.

The second quadrant and those that follow are also divided into right and left mode techniques. The development of both right and left mode functioning continues throughout the learning cycle. Some of our students are right mode dominant, some are left mode dominant, but all need to develop both types of problem solving skills.

The skills that are addressed in Quadrant Two include patterning, organizing and analyzing skills:

seeing relationships and interrelationships, identifying parts, ordering, prioritizing, classifying, and comparing.

Reflective
Observation
(Watching/Reflecting)

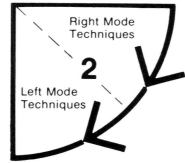

Abstract
Conceptualization
(Thinking/Developing Concepts)

**Reflective
Observation**

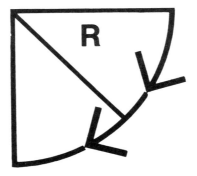

**Abstract
Conceptualization**

Quadrant Two: Concept Formulation

Step Three

Integrating Observations into Concepts

Type Two, Right Mode Learner most comfortable
Teacher Role — Teacher
Method — Informational
Question to be answered — What?
"Teach it to them."

Read the poem, "Casey at the Bat"

*The outlook wasn't brilliant for the Mudville
nine that day,
The score stood four to two, with but one
inning more to play;
And so, when Cooney died at first, and
Barrows did the same,
A sickly silence fell upon the patrons
of the game.*

*A straggling few got up to go in deep despair,
the rest
Clung to the hope which springs eternal in the
human breast;
They thought, if only Casey could but get
a whack, at that,
They'd put up even money now, with Casey
at the bat.*

*But Flynn preceded Casey, as did also
Jimmy Blake,
And the former was a pudding and the latter
was a fake;
So upon that stricken multitude grim
melancholy sat,
For there seemed but little chance of Casey's
getting to the bat.*

But Flynn let drive a single, to the
wonderment of all,
And Blake, the much despised, tore the cover
off the ball;
And when the dust had lifted, and they saw
what had occurred,
There was Jimmy safe on second, and Flynn
a-hugging third.

Then from the gladdened multitude went up a
joyous yell,
It bounded from the mountain-top, and
rattled in the dell;
It struck upon the hillside, and recoiled
upon the flat;
For Casey, mighty Casey, was advancing
to the bat.

There was ease in Casey's manner as he
stepped into his place,
There was pride in Casey's bearing, and a
smile on Casey's face;
And when, responding to the cheers, he
lightly doffed his hat,
Not stranger in the crowd could doubt 'twas
Casey at the bat.

Ten thousand eyes were on him as he rubbed
his hands with dirt,
Five thousand tongues applauded when he
wiped them on his shirt;
Then while the writhing pitcher ground the
ball into his hip,
Defiance gleamed in Casey's eye, a sneer
curled Casey's lip.

And now the leather-covered sphere came
hurtling through the air,
And Casey stood a-watching it in haughty
grandeur there;
Close by the sturdy batsman the ball
unheeded sped.

"That ain't my style," said Casey. "Strike one,"
the umpire said.

From the benches, black with people, there
went up a muffled roar,
Like the beating of the storm-waves on a
stern and distant shore;
"Kill him! kill the umpire!" shouted some one
on the stand.
And it's likely they'd have killed him had not
Casey raised his hand.

With a smile of Christian charity great Casey's
visage shone;
He stilled the rising tumult; he bade the
game go on;
He signalled to the pitcher, and once more
the spheroid flew,
But Casey still ignored it, and the umpire said,
"Strike two."

"Fraud!" cried the maddened thousands, and
the echo answered, "Fraud!"
But a scornful look from Casey, and the
audience was awed;
They saw his face grow stern and cold,
they saw his muscles strain,
And they knew that Casey wouldn't let that
ball go by again.

The sneer is gone from Casey's lips, his teeth
are clenched in hate;
He pounds with cruel violence his bat upon
the plate;
And now the pitcher holds the ball, and now
he lets it go,
And now the air is shattered by the force of
Casey's blow.

Oh! somewhere in this favored land the sun is shining bright,
The band is playing somewhere, and some-where hearts are light;
And somewhere men are laughing, and some-where children shout,
But there is no joy in Mudville — mighty Casey has struck out.

After reading the poem to the class, emphasize two aspects in discussing it.

1. visual imagery — the ability to see pictures in one's mind, formed by the poet's words.
2. arousing feelings — remind the class how they felt when they watched the skits, how distressing it would be to be Casey. Pulling from the skits, remind them of how the "coaches" felt about Casey.

Point out the relationship between the experience skits (Step One) they created and performed and reiterate some of their comments made during the analysis discussion (Step Two). *Integrate* Steps One and Two with the actual poem (Step Three), the presentation of the material.

Comments on Step Three

This is a right mode step: the *integration* of the experience and the reflections on the experience with the material to be presented. The right mode, Type Two Learner is most comfortable when integrating reflections on experience into developing concepts. This calls forth a synthesis of Steps One, Two, and Three. It paves the way for the more technical aspects of poetry analyses which follow in Step Four.

While some discussion will be necessary to check out the connections the students are making in this step, the teacher is the primary actor, pulling it all together. The method is informational, but the information is based on an experience the class has had, and the information presented includes the class reactions to that experience.

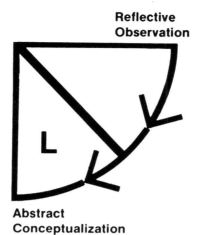

Reflective Observation

L

Abstract Conceptualization

Step Four

Developing Theories and Concepts

Type Two, Left Mode Learner most comfortable
Teacher Role — Teacher
Method — Informational
Question to be answered — What?
"Teach it to them."

Teach them:

Meter
Onomatopoeia
Alliteration
Metaphor
Simile

Have them list in their notebooks all vocabulary words in the poem which they do not know.

Then have each child go to the board and write two unknown words, until all words are listed.

Comments on Step Four

Now the teacher presents the "acknowledged knowledge," the actual techniques that go into writing poetry. The students are asked to examine the poem in light of these techniques. The left mode characteristic of Step Four lies in the breaking down of the material into its parts, and the examination and analyses of those parts.

The left mode, Type Two Learner is very comfortable in this step. "What?" is the question these students want answered. "What do the experts say I need to know to understand poetry?"

Any good poetry text could be used to assist the teacher in this phase. Paramount in quadrant two is the organizational skill of the teacher, who must present the material in sequential form.

It is Step Four that is most often presented in our schools, usually exclusively. It is a vital step because "acknowledged knowledge" forms a standard of excellence that must be kept uppermost in presenting any material, but it is simply not enough. We must encourage the diversity of perceiving and processing knowledge and experience by allowing the four different learning style approaches to be realized. To present only Step Four (and Step Five, the manipulation of fixed materials and concepts, which follows) is to teach exclusively to those students who fall on the Abstract Conceptualization end of the perception continuum, thereby ignoring the needs of the other students.

The Third Quadrant
Practice and Personalization

A process of learning from
Abstract Conceptualization to
Active Experimentation,
Thinking/Developing Concepts to Doing/
Trying it Themselves.

All of the students continue on through this process, but quadrant three appeals most to the Common Sense Learners.

The Type Three Learner's most comfortable place is the lower left corner of the model.

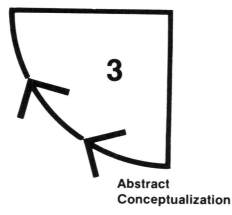

**Active
Experimentation**

3

**Abstract
Conceptualization**

Teacher Role = Coach

Method = Facilitation

Common Sense Learners rely heavily on kinetic involvement to learn, using body senses as a focus for understanding. They need to *try it.* They are concerned with finding out the answer to the question, "How does this work?" They are anxious to try it themselves. They edit reality. The teacher's role is to provide the materials and the encouragement necessary for a "trying things out" environment.

Abraham Maslow speaks of growth as taking place subjectively, "from within outward." He comments on the healthy child as follows:

> . . . he tends to try out his powers, to reach out, to be absorbed, fascinated, interested, to play, to wonder, to manipulate the world. **Exploring, manipulating, experiencing,** being interested, choosing . . .
>
> (This) lead(s) to Becoming through a serendipitous way, fortuitously, unplanned, unanticipated. Spontaneous, creative experience can and does happen without expectations, plans, foresight, purpose or goal.

In commenting on the relationship between safety and growth, Maslow goes on to say:

> Apparently growth forward customarily takes place in little steps, and each step forward is made possible by the feeling of being safe, of operating out into the unknown from a **safe home port** (emphasis mine) of daring because retreat is possible . . . Now, how can we know when the child feels safe enough to dare to choose the new step ahead? Ultimately the only way in which we can know is by **his** choice which is to say only he can ever really know the right moment when the beckoning forces ahead overbalance the beckoning

forces behind, and courage outweighs fear.
Ultimately the person, even the child must
choose for himself. Nobody can choose for
him too often, for this itself enfeebles him,
*cutting his self-trust, and confusing his **ability***
to perceive his own internal delight in the
*experience, his **own** impulses, judgments,*
and feelings, and to differentiate them from
the interiorized standards of others.[2]

Maslow speaks eloquently of choices encouraged by a safe environment. I emphatically agree. I do not believe learning can take place without students being allowed to make choices, to explore, to manipulate, to experience. These activities are often found in primary schools, but exploration, manipulation, experimentation in the higher grades is frequently limited to reading another book, or writing another essay. Activities that appeal to only 25% of our students.

The skills that are addressed in quadrant three include experimenting, manipulating materials and building on givens, skills at which Type Three Common Sense Learners excel.

The four quadrants in the 4Mat System move from teacher initiated to student initiated activities. In quadrant one (Steps One and Two), the teacher is the initiator, the primary actor. S/he plans and implements the experience as well as the analysis discussion that follows the experience. In quadrant two, the teacher is the information giver; first in Step Three by pulling the experience and the analysis into the concepts to be taught, and secondly (Step Four) by "teaching" the material and skills.

This changes as we move into quadrant three. The third quadrant is where the students become active, more self-initiating. Students become the primary actors even more in quadrant four.

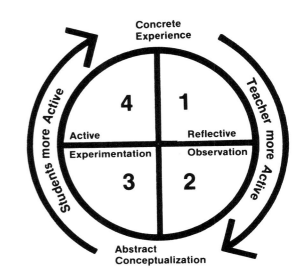

In the first quadrant the teacher creates a reason.

In the second quadrant the teacher teaches it to them.

In the third quadrant the teacher lets them try it themselves.[3]

The teacher's role in the third quadrant is one of coach/facilitator. The crucial teaching skill in this quadrant is organizational, to gather the materials needed for manipulation and to set up the encouraging environment needed so the students can try it themselves. Without the active involvement of the students, schooling is a sterile overlay, an externally applied act, satisfying the teacher perhaps (after all, s/he's working), but not involving the students in any meaningful way.

Whenever I present the 4Mat System to audiences and get to the third quadrant, I see and feel hesitancy. Teachers visualize noise and lack of control when they imagine a classroom where students are trying it themselves. This is not the case. Active involvement of students is *not* synonymous with noise and lack of control. The exact opposite is true. The more diverse the activities going on in a classroom at any single time, the more peace and quiet is necessary for concentration.

How do you retain peace and quiet? You facilitate, you make order possible. You teach small group work rules, you explain the use and care of diverse materials, you convince them that the rights of others must be maintained. These procedures must be taught, and when they begin to slip, the teacher should stop and draw the attention of the class to these rules again. With proper, patient training, a classroom where children are "engaged" is a quiet classroom.

So, the emphasis in the third quadrant (and the fourth) is on student activity. The students take the concepts and skills that have been taught and try them.

The third quadrant is also divided into Left and Right Mode Techniques.

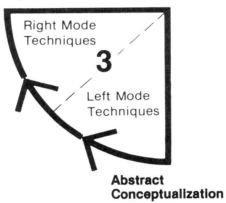

Active Experimentation

Right Mode Techniques

3

Left Mode Techniques

Abstract Conceptualization

Note that Left Mode techniques come first in the third quadrant.

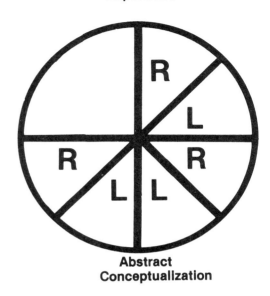

Concrete Experience

Abstract Conceptualization

This is because of the proximity to the *Abstract Conceptualization* dimension. As we move into quadrant three (Step Five) the students react to the "givens" presented in quadrant two, but in a more fixed, prearranged way than in Step Six.

The skills that are addressed in Quadrant Three are inquiring, exploring, and problem-solving skills:

experimenting, seeing, predicting, tinkering, recording, and making things work.

**Active
Experimentation**

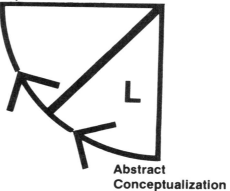

L

**Abstract
Conceptualization**

PLANS

Step Five
Working on Defined Concepts
(Reinforcement and Manipulation)

Type Three, Left Mode Learner most comfortable
Teacher Role — Coach
Method — Facilitation
Question to be answered — How does this work?
"Let them try it."

Work sheets on:
Meter, Onomatopoeia, Alliteration, Metaphor, Simile. Each child looks up the vocabulary words (two each) and writes their meaning on the board.

Vocabulary list: brilliant, eternal, striken, multitude, melancholy, wonderment, gladdened, dell, flat, bearing, doffed, writhing, defiance, sneer, haughty, grandeur, muffled, visage, tumult, spheroid, fraud, scornful, clenched.

Baseball slang: "died at first" "was a pudding" "safe on second" "a-hugging third" "ground the ball into his hip"

Comments on Step Five

In Step Five, the students react to the givens. They do work sheets, use work books, etc. These materials are used to reinforce the concepts and skills taught in quadrant two. A good poetry workbook of prepared exercises can be used in Step Five. This is a traditional step, as is Step Four. Steps Four and Five in the 4Mat model are usually attempted in our schools.

Note that these two steps, steps four and five, are left mode techniques. Step Four appeals to the Analytic left mode learners, and Step Five appeals to the Common Sense left mode learners. One can easily see the value of these two steps for *all* learners, but the exclusive teaching in only these two modes make it extremely difficult for any other type of learner to succeed. Schools must stop teaching exclusively in these two modes if we are to individualize in any meaningful way.

The left mode characteristic of Step Five lies in the reaction to givens. The students have been taught a skill, or a concept, and now they are asked to manipulate materials based on those skills/concepts. They are still adapting to experts, they are still working on prescribed materials. They have begun. But the creative stepping out, the adding something of their own, the applying their own uniqueness to the material, comes in Step Six, the right mode step of quadrant three.

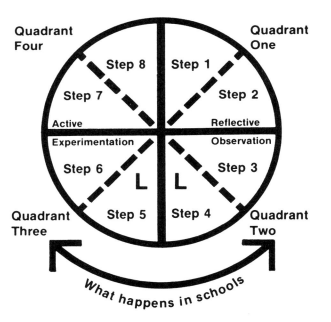

**Active
Experimentation**

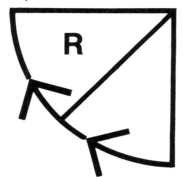

R

**Abstract
Conceptualization**

*Quadrant Three:
Practice and Personalization*

Step Six
"Messing Around"
(Adding Something of Themselves)

Type Three, Right Mode Learner most comfortable
Teacher Role — Coach
Method — Facilitation
Question to be answered — How does this work?
"Let them try it."

Self chosen groups:

One group brainstorms TV commercials that use the theme of losing, then show losers getting a lift from some product: Mean Joe Greene and Coke — Lifesavers and the hockey player with his dad after losing, etc.

One group reads other poems about losers and winners at different reading levels.

Examples: "Women" "Taught Me Purple"
"Follower" "Paradigm of a Hero"
"Youth" "The Base Stealer" "Cobb
Would have Caught it" "Mother
to Son"[4]

One group gathers pictures from magazines of winners and losers for collages.

One group makes and posts colorful, "arty" lists of vocabulary words learned.

One group examines the lyrics of songs about winning and losing: "Eleanor Rigby" "Even Losers Win Sometimes" etc.

Baseball, basketball paintings
Talk to PE teacher about setting up a game
Writing their own poems
A film on sports and ethics

Comments on Step Six

By now it is obvious to the reader that much more than "Casey at the Bat" is being taught in this unit. Casey is a means, a vehicle to engage the students, especially the students who feel poetry is for "sissies." A poem such as Casey dispels that image. ("The Cremation of Sam McGee" is also a great introduction to poetry for older students.) With material that has so many possibilities, why do we ever bore our students? Even punctuation rules, surely as mundane as one can get, can be fun and filled with diversity. (See the punctuation lesson plan for the primary grades in Part Four).

Nothing is boring and mundane.

Children know that when they are small, but we take their wonder away.

Real integration begins with Step Six:

personality interests, skills unique to students, as well as media integration.

In Step Six, the students are "adding something of themselves," "messing around," and making the material theirs.

The right mode characteristic of Step Six is in the integration of the material and the self, the personal synthesis, as well as in the opportunity for students to approach the content in their own most comfortable way. The right mode Common Sense Learners are most comfortable in Step Six.

To return to Maslow:

If the child can **choose** *the experiences which are validated by the experience of delight, then he can return to the experience, repeat it, savor it to the point of repletion, satiation or boredom. At this point he shows the tendency to go on to more complex, richer experiences and accomplishments.*

. . . Such experiences not only mean moving on, but have a feedback effect on the Self, in the feeling of certainty ("This I like; that I don't for **sure***"); of capability, mastery, self-trust, self-esteem.*[5]

Learning is a Ladder *and* a Spiral.

The Fourth Quadrant
Integrating Application and Experience

A process of learning from
Active Experimentation to Concrete Experience,
Doing/Trying It Themselves to Sensing/Feeling.

All of the students go through this process, but quadrant four appeals most to the Dynamic Learners.

The Type Four Dynamic Learner's most comfortable place is the upper left corner of the model.

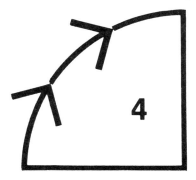

Concrete Experience

Active Experimentation

Teacher's Role = Evaluator/Remediator

Method = Self Discovery

The Dynamic Learner is outgoing and relies on intuition as a primary focus for understanding. Dynamic Learners "test the air" by combining knowledge gained from personal experience and experimentation. They want to know "What can this become?" "What can I make of this?" They enrich reality.

They need to learn on their own. These characteristics make them difficult students if their teachers (and parents) interpret these needs as lack of control or disrespect.

Quite the contrary, they listen to experts, but they continually check out what experts say in light of their own experiences. With a stimulating environment and with proper guidance they are tenacious in their concentration. When they are excited about something they are working on, they appear to be deaf and dumb to the world around them. Because their focus is the self, when they are into something, they are really into it. And when they are encouraged to question their own intuitions and actions, they do so with increased self-awareness.

The teacher's role in quadrant four is that of evaluator-remediator. This is the creative part of teaching, where one must be able to guide and prod, to encourage and challenge.

In the first quadrant the teacher *created a reason;*
In the second quadrant the teacher *taught it to them;*
in the third quadrant the teacher *let them try it themselves;*
in the fourth quadrant the teacher must *let them teach it to themselves and to others.*

By the time teachers get to Steps Seven and Eight (quadrant four), their role is vastly changed from the earlier steps. The students are now at the point where they can show what they have learned in *their own best ways.* The teacher is evaluating and remediating. This is the point where the students can be of great help to each other. Since many activities can be chosen, depending on the student's learning style (this is delineated in Step Eight), many opportunities for sharing exist in this phase of the learning cycle. The teacher's task is to reinforce and guide. Some of the students will need more help than others. Some will need to work on their own. In this phase, the evaluation should be twofold:

1. basic materials all must master
2. unique "proofs" of learning chosen by the students themselves.

I can hear the groans. How much easier to give one objective test of facts to all, and how easily corrected. Fine for the basics, but how unfair to expect all the children to prove their mastery in the same way. Remember that you are dealing with four learning styles and right and left brain dominance. The evaluation techniques used are crucial to the students' beliefs that alternative modes of learning are equally valued.

If you have followed the model, the students have "gone around the circle."

You created an experience (right mode)
　You helped them reflect on that experience (left mode)
　　you helped them integrate their experience and their reflections into the material to be presented (right mode)
　　　you taught them the content/ skills (left mode)
　　　　you set up the resources and procedures so they could "add something of themselves" (right mode)

and now you are asking the students to *do* something with what they have learned.

You have created the motivation,
　You have taught emotional and thinking skills,
　　taught the basics,
　　　and let them practice.

You have "gone around the circle."

If you encourage only students who choose a traditional option (reading three other poems and writing an essay, for example) your message is loud and clear. You only value conventional learning. You're comfortable only with a small range of your students' potential.

We must let all students be themselves.
We must add to their experiences.
We must let them grow from within.

"Each bit of active experiencing is an opportunity toward finding out what s/he likes or dislikes, and more and more what s/he wants to make out of him/herself. It is an essential part of the progress toward the stage of maturity and self-direction." [6]

Quadrant four is also divided into left and right mode techniques. Step Seven is left mode and Step Eight is right mode.

The skills that are addressed in Quadrant Four include intergrating and evaluating skills:

verifying, explaining, summarizing, synthesizing, re-presenting, and re-focusing.

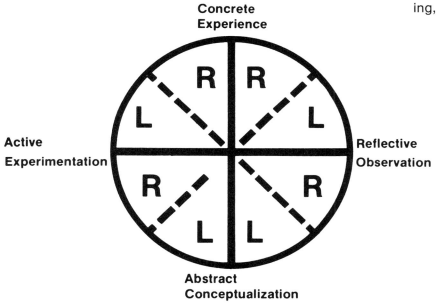

Concrete Experience

Active Experimentation

Reflective Observation

Abstract Conceptualization

Concrete Experience

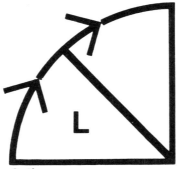

Active Experimentation

Quadrant Four:
Integrating Application and Experience

Step Seven
Analyzing for Usefulness or Application

Type Four, Left Mode Learner most comfortable
Teacher Role — Evaluator/Remediator
Method — Self-Discovery
Questions to be answered —What can this
become?
What can I make
of this?

"Let them teach it to themselves and to someone else."

Each student writes his/her own essay on what can be learned from a good poem.

Each student writes a plan for doing his/her own "Casey at the Bat."

The plan can be mimes, collages, poems of his/her own, TV commercials of his/her own, skits of his/her own,

or choosing other poems s/he would like to read to the class.

Students hand in these essays and plans.

Comments on Step Seven

This is the step where the students are asked to analyze what they have planned as their "proof" of learning. This analysis should be based on

1. relevance to the content/skills and
2. originality.

Step Seven requires the students to apply what they have learned in some personal, meaningful way. As you will see in the lesson plan samples in Part Four of this book, there are many different ways to achieve this step. Many kinds of choices are possible. For some units the students have to choose from one of only four options; for others there are many choices. Some of the factors that would dictate this include the number of students, the amount of time, and how accustomed the students are to having choices.

The students' *written* plans are all subject to the teacher's approval.

The left mode characteristic of Step Seven lies in the analysis of the planning.

**Concrete
Experience**

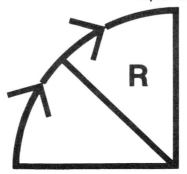

R

**Active
Experimentation**

Quadrant Four:
Integrating Application and Experience

Step Eight
*Doing It Themselves and
Sharing What They Do With Others*

Type Four, Right Mode Learner most comfortable
Teacher Role — Evaluator/Remediator
Method — Self-Discovery
Questions to be answered —"How can I apply
this?"
"What can this
become?"

"Let them teach it to themselves and to
someone else."

The students make their own "Casey at the Bat."

The students share what they have done with
each other.

End unit with the poem, "The Glow Within," to
encourage them that it is not winning or losing,
but what we have inside, that counts.

The Glow Within *

Oh, you gotta get a glory
In the work you do;
A hallelujah chorus
In the heart of you.
Paint, or tell a story,
Sing, or shovel coal,
But you gotta get a glory,
Or the job lacks soul.

Oh, Lord, give me a glory,
Is it much to give?
For you gotta get a glory
Or you just don't live!

The Great, whose shining labors
Make our pulses throb,
Were (wo)men who got a glory
In their daily job.
The battle might be gory
And the odds unfair,
But the (wo)men who got a glory
Never knew despair.

Oh, Lord, give me a glory.
When all else is gone,
If you've only got a glory
You can still go on!

To those who get a glory
It is like the sun,
And you can see it glowing
Through the work they've done.
Oh, fame is transitory,
Riches fade away,
But when you get a glory
It is there to stay.

Oh, Lord, give me a glory
And a workman's pride,
For you gotta get a glory
Or you're dead inside!

                    Berton Braley

Comments on Step Eight

Now the diversity really shows.
The students share and watch.
They listen to each other.
They see the diversity of creativity,
and they are learning that everyone's gifts
are valuable.
They are ready to go back "around the circle"
in ever increasing complexity.
They're learning the beautiful truth
that we all "shine"
some of the time.

* From *Reading-Literature, Book Three Revised;*
White Plains, New York: ©Row, Peterson and
Company. 1955. 186.

The Complete
4Mat System Model

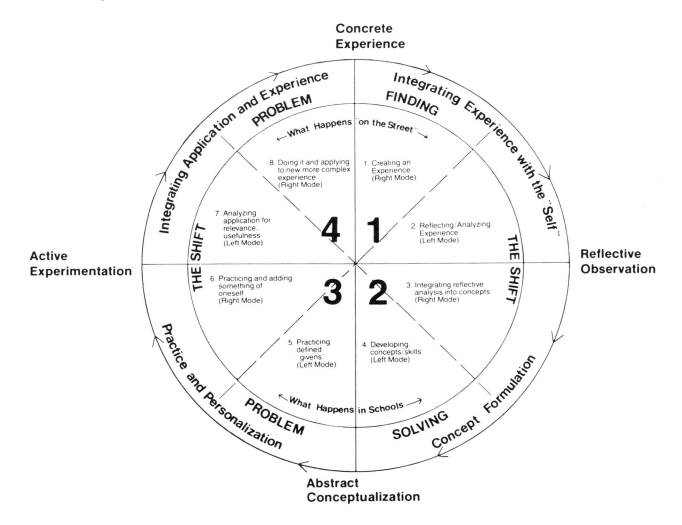

By beginning at the top of the model with Concrete Experience and moving clockwise, we have a curricular progression that includes all four learning styles and uses right and left mode techniques. This progression is an effective, common sense method of learning.

Quadrant One: Integrating Experience with the Self

1. Create a concrete experience. Right Mode

2. Reflect on experience, analyze it. Left Mode

Quadrant Two: Concept Formulation

3. Integrate experience and reflections into concepts. Right Mode

4. Examine and formulate concepts. Left Mode

Quadrant Three: Practice and Personalization

5. Work on defined concepts and givens. Left Mode

6. "Mess around" with givens. Add something of themselves. Right Mode

Quadrant Four: Integrating Application and Experience

7. Analyze application, judge results of experimentation. Left Mode

8. Apply learning personally and share with others. Right Mode

Then back to new richer experiences (the Concrete Experience Stage again) armed with skills gained by moving "around the circle."

This translates into teaching practice in the following way:

Imaginative Learners

Create a reason "Why or why not?"
Create an experience   Right Mode
Analyze that experience   Left Mode

Analytic Learners
Teach it to them   "What?"
Integrate the experience into the materials Right Mode
Give them the facts/skills   Left Mode

Common Sense Learners
Let them try it   "How does this work?"
Give them prepared materials   Left Mode
Let them create materials of their own Right Mode

Dynamic Learners
Let them teach it to themselves and someone else
"What can this become?"
"What can I make of this?"
Analyze their creations for relevance and originality   Left Mode
Do it and share with each other   Right Mode

I have labeled the bottom two-eighths of the circle "what happens in school." Almost all schools present concepts and skills and ask the students to practice the "givens."

Both steps are external.
Both steps involve the teacher.

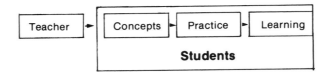

Students

Both steps are Left Mode.

I have labeled the top two-eighths of the circle "what happens on the street." All our students have experiences and they integrate these experiences (whether for good or bad) into their person. They internalize. They take the integrated experiences and then apply them to new experiences.

Both steps are internal.
The student is the main actor.

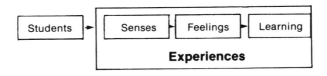

Experiences

To exclusively analyze, without personal involvement based on one's own perceptions, is to miss the human attributes of feeling, to deny the sensory perceptions that come from immersing oneself in the actual.

To exclusively experience and sense, without abstract analysis, is to deny the past, the intellectual achievements of mankind.

We must do both!

I have also labeled the bottom two-eighths of the circle, the two Left Mode steps on either side of the Abstract dimension, problem-solving. Schools really do try to do this. They give students concepts and then have them practice. The thinking through of a concept or problem requires analytical tools. This process is a *reaction*. People need to be taught to solve problems.

However, the top half of the circle, problem-finding, is not used in any systematic, conscious way in schools or training programs. Problem-finding is anticipatory. It is nonjudgmental, in the sense that it considers the flux of events. It can even be described as a random gathering of data, *both* experientially and intuitively. It leads to the consideration of better questions.

The ability to problem-find *cannot* be fruitful when logical analysis is lacking. When this is the case, patterns cannot be filtered out and acted upon. One just moves from one insight to another without the benefit of increasing one's decision-making ability. However, if one is trained "to keep moving around the circle" then problem-finding becomes that unique ability to integrate application and experience. It results from brainstorming, designing solutions, building these solutions into the system, trying them out, and analyzing their results in an ever-widening spiral. It is in "the shift" between problem-solving and problem-finding that we combine the four strengths inherent in the four learning styles. It is in the shift that we integrate left and right mode functioning.

The "shift" comes from taking experience and reflecting on it, analyzing it, developing it into an integration with acknowledged knowledge.

The "shift" also comes when one takes defined concepts (based on experiences and reflections) and tries them out, personally getting involved and then analyzing this personal involvement.

Schools must structure learning to bring about these "shifts," these integrations.

In *quadrant one,* the teacher's role is one of Motivator/Witness, in which s/he expresses through word and action the value of the learning experience personally. This should be done as part of the analysis of the created experience. The teacher must have a reason to teach as well as the learners need a reason to learn. The primary task of the teacher in quadrant one is to create an accepting climate where the imaginative learner (and all types of learners) can explore ideas without being evaluated too quickly. In order to accomplish this the teacher must create an experience where the students can see the reason for proceeding.

In *quadrant two,* the teacher's role is that of Information Giver, the traditional role of the teacher. S/he must present data in an organized way, leading students to analyze data and form concepts.

In *quadrant three,* the teacher's role is that of Facilitator/Coach. The teacher steps back and is available as a coach and stabilizer in the activities of the students.

In *quadrant four,* the teacher's role is that of Evaluator/Remediator, creating a climate where there is freedom to discover by doing. The teacher challenges the students to look at what has happened, analyze it for relevance and originality, do it, and share it with others. It is here that s/he steps in to evaluate and to help those students who need more.

Summing Up

In implementing the 4Mat System it is key for the teacher to:

1. Recognize his/her own dominant learning style and how this affects teaching styles.

2. Stretch into using methodologies that are suited to different learning styles. Take one step at a time, and remember to take into account your own tolerance for testing new methods.

3. Observe and discuss with students what their dominant learning styles are.

4. Value each learning style as equally important.

5. Encourage and allow opportunities for students to teach one another through demonstrating their dominant modes.

6. Become acquainted with the research on right and left brain dominance.

7. Become aware of your own brain dominance.

8. Use both right and left techniques in your classroom.

The Teacher's Role: A Recapitulation

The teacher's role changes as s/he moves
through the cycle of learning:
from Motivator/Witness
    to Teacher/Information Giver
        to Facilitator/Coach
            to Evaluator/Remediator and
Resource.

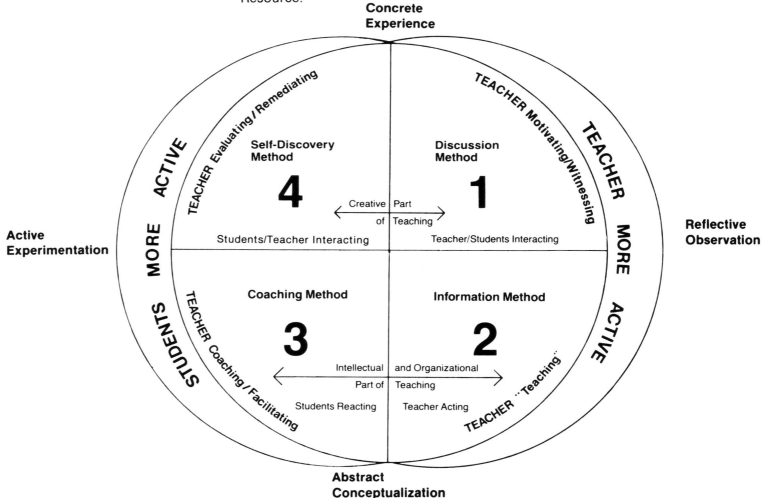

★ Create a reason,

　★ teach it to them,

　　★ let them try it
　　adding something of themselves,

　　　★　and let them teach it to themselves
　　　and share with others.

Developing and integrating all four modes of learning and developing and integrating both right and left brain processing skills should be a major goal of education. Through this process, students can come to accept their strengths and learn to capitalize on them. At the same time, they can develop a healthy respect for the uniqueness of others and further their abilities to learn in alternative modes without the pressure of "being wrong."

Educators must continue to search for more potent methods of discovering individual skills and learning preferences. It is imperative that we incorporate methodologies that speak to all of our students. We must structure learning so learners can teach each other. In a recent class in law-related education, the drinking age was raised as a topic because the drinking age in the vicinity had just been raised back up to 21. The Analytic Learners got involved in the statistical reasons, insurance rates, accident levels; the Common Sense Learners went out "on the street" and interviewed bartenders, parents, and students their own age; the Innovative Learners did a unit on alcoholism (personal meaning — so many of our students experience the tragedy of alcohol in their families); the Dynamic Learners interviewed legislators and rewrote the law. (The improved law *also* moved the drinking age back up to 21.) The students learned from each other. The statistics without the street survey were just statistics, and the street survey without the facts and statistics was just a small personal experience. But the combination was stunning.

Adding Modalities

In honoring the four major
learning styles
and left- and right-mode processing
preferences,
we need to teach to
Modalities.

Modalities are the sensory channels
by which we receive information.

VISUAL
Colors, images, shapes, drawings,
paintings, patterns, forms,
sculpture

AUDITORY
Hearing, vibrations, rhythms,
mentally configured sounds,
patterns, tone, oral directions,
chanting and listening

KINESTHETIC
Body movements, dance,
gesturing, hula-ing, positioning,
touching—all physical action

A person learns visually by seeing.

Visual Modalities are those which are activated by
input or output using visual/spatial expression
such as art, sculpture, mapping, graphics, and
other forms of visually dominated expression.

A person learns auditorially by hearing.

Auditory Modalities are those which are activated
by input or output in the use of patterned sound.
Speech is the earliest formal expression of these
modalities but music, song and
rhythmic awareness are also primary.

**A person learns kinesthetically by
moving and touching.**

Kinesthetic Modalities are those which are excited
by input and output involving movement.
Movement is fundamental to basic human
understanding, and patterned movement and
dance are the core of much human learning.

A well-written 4MAT lesson will, by its very nature, include modalities. So much so, in fact, that one strong way to evaluate a 4MAT lesson is for its inclusion of modalities.

The reasons are inherent in the nature of the 4MAT Model itself.

Modality activities tend to be holistic. They have a gestalt sensitivity. They are related to right-mode processing. The following are but a few examples. Readers are urged to read Bradshaw and Nettleton, 1983.

Visual:

The Right Mode is superior at perceiving the relationships between component parts and the whole. (Nebes, 1978)

The Right Mode is superior at forming a complete gestalt (e.g., a circle) from incomplete information (e.g., arcs of a circle). (Nebes, 1978)

The Right Mode is superior at processing faces. (Bradshaw, 1983)

Auditory:

The Right Mode is superior at mediating musical processing. (Bogen and Gordon, 1971)

The Right Mode plays a major role in singing. (Gordon, 1974)

While musical functions are not strictly lateralized to the Right Hemisphere, there may often be a considerable Right Hemisphere involvement. (Bradshaw, 1983)

Kinesthetic:

There is Right Mode (left hand) superiority in reading Braille. (Bradshaw, 1983)

There is a strong Right Mode involvement in signing (language of the deaf). (Cutting, 1980)

There is a Right Mode superiority in the tactile perception of spatial relationships. (Whitaker and Ojemann, 1977)

Students have modality preferences. Although most of us use multiple modalities, research shows that we **do** favor some over others.

And some learners tend to have a strong dominance in one modality.

A study of 600 children in grades Kindergarten to 6 showed: [7]

Visual Dominance: 33%
Auditory Dominance: 24%
Kinesthetic Dominance: 14%
Mixed Modalities: 29%

A visual learner learns by seeing and imagining.

An auditory learner learns by listening and verbalizing.

A kinesthetic learner learns by doing and manipulating.

All learners can profit by the use of multiple and mixed modality instructional techniques.

Part Four

Sample
Lesson Plans

Primary Units

AUTHOR: BERNICE McCARTHY

THEME: "It was from my own early experience that I decided there was no use to which money could be applied so productive of good to boys and girls who have good within them and ability and ambition to develop it as the funding of a public library." Andrew Carnegie

QUADRANT ONE

INTEGRATING EXPERIENCE WITH THE SELF

THE IMAGINATIVE LEARNER'S MOST COMFORTABLE PLACE

CONCERN WITH PERSONAL MEANING — CREATE A REASON

Answer the question "WHY?"

Teacher's Role — Motivator

Method — Simulation to encourage brainstorming for imagination, innovation, and empathy

---

1. Right Mode

Create An Experience

Teacher More Active

Objective:

To help students truly believe that reading is fun. To capitalize on the innate need for self-expression.

To help students enjoy listening to reading.

Activity:

"Experience Stories." This is an old, traditional technique, and a good one. A child has a happy experience, s/he tells the class or teacher about it. The teacher writes the story in two or three simple sentences on large paper. The child illustrates "his/her" story on the same paper, then begins learning the words.

Experiences can also be created in the classroom so the class can write a story together.

Draw symbol stories[1]

house   sun   flower   tree

Read to them every day. (See punctuation unit, pages 137 to 140, for reasons people write things down).

Evaluation:

Listening, being engaged, enjoying.

2. Left Mode

Analyze The Experience

Teacher More Active

Objective:

To take the time to discuss what reading is for. To have them share their feelings about the fun of listening to a good story.

Activity:

Read your best story. Start a discussion about how they like to hear a good story.

Evaluation:

Participation in the discussion.

QUADRANT TWO

CONCEPT FORMULATION

THE ANALYTIC LEARNER'S MOST
COMFORTABLE PLACE

CONCERN FOR THE FACTS AS EXPERTS SEE
THEM — TEACH IT TO THEM

Answer the question "WHAT?"

Teacher's Role — Information Giver

Method — Informational

---

3. Right Mode

Integrate Reflections Into Concepts

Teacher More Active

Objective:

To connect symbols and sounds to meanings.
This is the crucial step. I call it the "water" step.
This refers to that beautiful moment in William
Gibson's play *The Miracle Worker*[2] when the
young Helen Keller connects the hand symbol
for water with water itself. *Be sure all the
children make this crucial connection, in as
many ways as you can.*

Activity:

One option: Have the children *be* simple words.
Put signs on the children, for example, the word
bat. Ask another child to stand next to the child

with the sign and *be* a bat, etc. Have the children
be letters. One child "b," another "a" (use the
dictionary symbols for sound right from the
beginning), and another "t." See if they can
match the configuration with the word by
looking at the child with the complete word "bat"
on his/her sign. This can be done later with
simple sentences and even short stories.

Evaluation:

Making the crucial connection between the
symbol and the meaning.

4. Left Mode

Develop Theories And Concepts

Teacher More Active

Objective:

To begin a serious study of sounds and letters.
To connect letter symbols to sounds and
meanings.

Activity:

Phonics, alphabet, spatial qualities, configurations.

Note:

The right mode children will need more time to
use their unique talent for spatial configuration.
It appears a modified "Look-Say" method has
real validity for certain students.

Beginning vocabulary. Use any good reading
series.

Evaluation:

Quality of understanding.

QUADRANT THREE

PRACTICE AND PERSONALIZATION

THE COMMON SENSE LEARNER'S MOST
COMFORTABLE PLACE

CONCERN FOR HANDS-ON EXPERIENCE —
LET THEM TRY IT

Answer the question "HOW DOES THIS WORK?"

Teacher's Role — Coach/Facilitator

Method — Facilitation

---

5. Left Mode

Working On Defined Concepts

(Reinforcement and Manipulation)

Students More Active

Objective:

To give practice in the concepts.

Activity:

Workbooks, worksheets made by teacher incorporating the vocabulary from each child's
experience story. Any good primary workbook
and text has many such activities.

Evaluation:

Quality of work.

6. Right Mode

"Messing Around"

(Adding Something of Themselves)

Students More Active

Objective:

To give right mode activities. Reading texts do not incorporate nearly enough right mode processing skills. They seem to stop short of including them. Some appear in primary texts, but they virtually disappear after fourth grade.

Activity:

Use tactile and kinetic methods: sandpaper letters, three dimensional letters, puzzles, pattern and configuration problems. Add movement (i.e., being letters, words, etc.), writing letters and words and symbols in clay, finger paint, sand, etc. Also use aural methods. One teacher I interviewed[3] discovered that a boy who had been unable to learn to read succeeded when she taped the stories and had him follow along with the book while listening to her voice through earphones.

Evaluation:

Quality of process.

QUADRANT FOUR

INTEGRATING APPLICATION AND EXPERIENCE

THE DYNAMIC LEARNER'S MOST COMFORTABLE PLACE

CONCERN FOR ACTION, DOING — LET THEM TEACH IT TO THEMSELVES AND SHARE WHAT THEY LEARN WITH OTHERS

Answer the questions
"WHAT CAN THIS BECOME?"
"WHAT CAN I MAKE OF THIS?"

Teacher's Role — Evaluator/Remediator

Method — Self-Discovery

---

7. Left Mode

Analyzing Their Own Application Of The Concepts For Usefulness, Originality, And As A Stepping Stone For Future Learning

Students More Active

Objective:

To give students practice in using what they have learned.

To help them examine the concepts and manipulate them.

Activity:

Have the children make worksheets, tape recordings etc. for each other. (Encourage them to use all methods and materials.)

Evaluation:

Quality of work.

8. Right Mode

Doing It Themselves And Sharing What They Do With Others

(Integrating Application and Experience)

Students More Active

Objective:

To share what they have learned.

Activity:

Have the children try out the materials they have made on each other.

Evaluation:

Participation and cooperation.

The Complete 4MAT System Model

Reading

Primary

Place to Begin
Concrete
Experience

Integrating Application and Experience
PROBLEM

Integrating Experience with the "Self"
FINDING

← What Happens "on the Street" →

Pupils try own materials
on
each other

Experience stories,
Listening,
Symbol stories

THE SHIFT

Pupils make their own
learning materials

4 **1**

Discussions on
reading as fun

THE SHIFT

Active
Experimentation

Reflective
Observation

THE SHIFT

Tactile and
kinetic methods

3 **2**

Physically *be* letters,
words.

Workbooks,
worksheets

Phonics,
alphabet,
configurations

Practice and Personalization

PROBLEM

← What Happens in Schools →

SOLVING

Concept Formulation

Abstract
Conceptualization

Subject: Language Arts   Unit: Punctuation   Grade Level: Primary

AUTHOR: BERNICE McCARTHY

THEME: "If you would learn to speak or write well, know when to pause, and when to finish."   Unknown

QUADRANT ONE

INTEGRATING EXPERIENCE WITH THE SELF

THE IMAGINATIVE LEARNER'S MOST COMFORTABLE PLACE

CONCERN WITH PERSONAL MEANING — CREATE A REASON

Answer the question "WHY?"

Teacher's Role — Motivator

Method — Simulation to encourage brainstorming for imagination, innovation, and empathy

---

1. Right Mode

Create An Experience

Teacher More Active

Objective:

To illustrate the need for punctuation in written language by relating it to pauses in spoken language.

Activity:

Choose a story written by one of the children. Comment: "I'm going to read Tom's wonderful story, but I'm going to change it. I want you to listen and see if you can tell me how I have changed it."

Read the story as though it had no punctuation.

Discuss what happened.

Choose four children to *be* punctuation marks: One a period, one a comma, one an exclamation mark, and one a question mark. Hang signs around their necks.

Choose a good reader and coach the student. Let him/her practice a few times. The teacher could prepare a simple passage in advance.

For example: Sally Pig and Kevin Frog went on a picnic in a beautiful yellow car it was a breezy sunny and warm day suddenly bang they had a flat tire Kevin Frog stopped the car he got out to fix the tire Sally Pig tried to help Kevin jack up the car and she pushed this way when she should have pushed that way the car fell knocking Kevin Frog into a big deep and muddy puddle alongside the road what do you think Sally Pig did next

This passage needs: 6 periods, 1 exclamation mark, 2 commas, and 1 question mark.

The children who are the punctuation marks stand in a straight line facing the class. The punctuation marks are told to listen to the story about to be read, and jump in when they think

they should. (Tell them to jump once forward.) The children in their seats are told to watch and decide if the punctuation marks have jumped in at the right time. If not, they get to take their place.

Have the passage read once while all listen. On the second reading, tell the punctuation marks to be ready.

Play the game. Have several other passages ready so more of the children get to play.

Evaluation:

Fun the children have.

2. Left Mode

Analyze The Experience

Teacher More Active

Objective:

To help them understand why we need the written word.

Activity:

Emphasize the purpose of writing things down.

Questions for the children:
If we could be everywhere at once and see all the things that are happening in the world, would we need to read about things?

If we could meet everyone in the world and talk to them and listen to what they have to say, would we need to read?

Emphasis: We only write things down so people can have a part of us when we are not there. Writing things down is a way of experiencing and remembering things people say about all kinds of things: about Sally Pig and Kevin Frog, about animals, about the stars and the mountains and the oceans, about the weather, about machines and about people.

When we talk, we have to pause so people can understand where one idea ends and another idea begins. That way people can understand what we mean.

Punctuation marks are only pauses in speech. They are places where we stop when we are reading so we can understand the end of one sentence and the beginning of another.

Divide the children into groups of five. Give each group a written passage of four to five sentences without punctuation. Be sure the passage needs a comma, an exclamation mark, and a question mark, as well as periods.

Instruct the children that: One of them must be the reader, one the period, one the comma, one the question mark, and one the exclamation mark.

Have them rotate in turn so that each child gets to play all five parts.

Evaluation:

Quality of the experience for the children.

QUADRANT TWO

CONCEPT FORMULATION

THE ANALYTIC LEARNER'S MOST COMFORTABLE PLACE

CONCERN FOR THE FACTS AS EXPERTS SEE THEM — TEACH IT TO THEM

Answer the question "WHAT?"

Teacher's Role — Information Giver

Method — Informational

---

3. Right Mode

Integrate Reflections Into Concepts

Teacher More Active

Objective:

To teach the concept of period, comma, exclamation mark, and question mark through the use of metaphor.

Activity:

Give each child a large piece of art paper.
— Instruct them to divide the paper into four sections.
— Tell them to draw four pictures:
— One of themselves stopping,
— one of themselves pausing,
— one of themselves being surprised,
— and one of themselves questioning.

Evaluation:

Quality of work in understanding the concepts.

4. Left Mode

Develop Theories Into Concepts

Teacher More Active

Objective:

To reteach and reinforce concepts of the period, comma, exclamation mark and question mark.

Activity:

Teacher instructs the children in proper use of above. Teacher can follow any good text and gear the information to needs of class.

Evaluation:

Quality of workbooks, worksheets, etc.

QUADRANT THREE

PRACTICE AND PERSONALIZATION

THE COMMON SENSE LEARNER'S MOST COMFORTABLE PLACE

CONCERN FOR HANDS-ON EXPERIENCE — LET THEM TRY IT

Answer the question "HOW DOES THIS WORK?"

Teacher's Role — Coach/Facilitator

Method — Facilitation

5. Left Mode

Working On Defined Concepts

(Reinforcement and Manipulation)

Students More Active

Objective:

To give further practice in use of punctuation marks.

Activity:

Workbooks accompanying texts, work sheets devised by teacher.

Evaluation:

Quality of above.

6. Right Mode

"Messing Around"

(Adding Something of Themselves)

Students More Active

Objective:

To personalize the learning so that students add something of themselves, do something with it.

Activity:

Children write their own stories without punctuation. (Tell them to suspend the use of capitals because that would give too strong a hint.)

Children hand in their stories to the teacher. On the back they state what punctuation marks are and where they are needed.

Evaluation:

Quality of stories and understanding of correct punctuation marks.

QUADRANT FOUR

INTEGRATING APPLICATION AND EXPERIENCE

THE DYNAMIC LEARNER'S MOST COMFORTABLE PLACE

CONCERN FOR ACTION, DOING — LET THEM TEACH IT TO THEMSELVES AND SHARE WHAT THEY LEARN WITH OTHERS

Answer the questions
"WHAT CAN THIS BECOME?"
"WHAT CAN I MAKE OF THIS?"

Teacher's Role — Evaluator/Remediator

Method — Self-Discovery

7. Left Mode

Analyzing Their Own Application Of The Concepts For Usefulness, Originality, And As A Stepping Stone For Future Learning

Students More Active

Objective:

To evaluate their understanding of the four punctuation marks taught and to remediate where necessary.

Activity:

Teacher hands back children's stories after checking them for accuracy. (Through this process teacher can find the children who need more help.)

Evaluation:

Accuracy of stories in terms of punctuation.

8. Right Mode

Doing It Themselves And Sharing What They Have Done With Others

(Integrating Application and Experience)

Students More Active

Objective:

To share their stories with each other.

Activity:

Assign each child a partner. Have them exchange stories. Each child inserts the proper punctuation. They correct each other's work.

They then rewrite their own stories inserting proper punctuation and capitalization.

Note:

Inform the music teacher when you are doing this unit so s/he can capitalize on this to teach musical rests.

Evaluation:

Participation and accuracy.

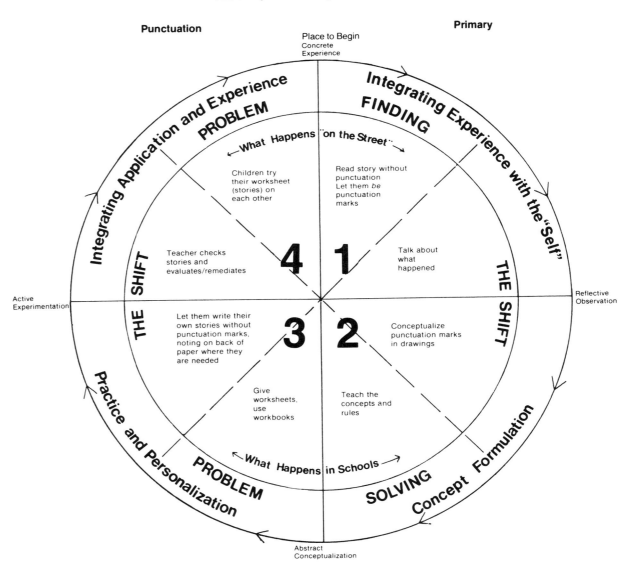

The Complete 4MAT System Model

140

AUTHOR: WILLIAM A. McCARTHY JR.

THEME: "The study of mathematics is like climbing up a steep and craggy mountain; when you reach the top, it fully recompenses your trouble, by opening a fine, clear, and extensive prospect."   Tryon Edwards

QUADRANT ONE

INTEGRATING EXPERIENCE WITH THE SELF

THE IMAGINATIVE LEARNER'S MOST COMFORTABLE PLACE

CONCERN WITH PERSONAL MEANING — CREATE A REASON

Answer the question "WHY?"

Teacher's Role — Motivator

Method — Simulation to encourage brainstorming for imagination, innovation, and empathy

---

1. Right Mode

Create An Experience

Teacher More Active

Objective:

To introduce/reinforce place value concept by allowing the children to *physically be* numbers.

Activity:

Draw two large circles on the floor. Make them large enough for nine children only. Draw two large squares on the blackboard directly above and behind each circle.

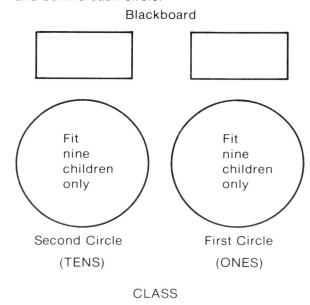

Blackboard

Second Circle   First Circle

(TENS)   (ONES)

CLASS

Give eleven children signs to wear, each with the number one on it.

Have one of the children with the signs go up and stand in the first circle (the ones circle). Ask the children how many people are standing in the first circle. When they answer "one" put a 1 in the large square on the blackboard directly behind and above the ones circle.

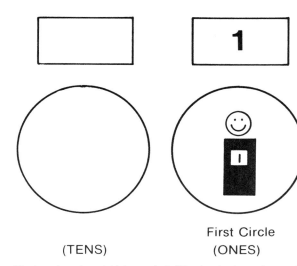

(TENS)   First Circle

         (ONES)

State clearly at this point "that what we have in the circle is one one." This is the switch that is crucial, to switch from "things" to number notation terminology.

Have another child go up and join the first child. Ask "How many ones do we have now?" When the answer is given, change the number 1 on the blackboard to number 2. And so on until you have nine children standing in the first circle. You *must* emphasize the distinctness of 2,3,4, etc. i.e.

otherwise some of them do not understand why nine (9) is not

It is of course simple to us, but they need to know why we use the integer symbols at all.

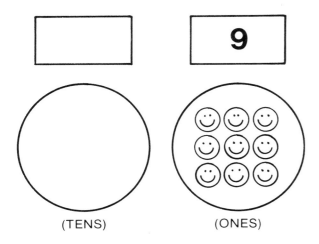

(TENS) (ONES)

"How many ones?" "Nine ones." Each time erase the previous number and put the next one in its place. When the tenth child tries to join the group, note to the class there isn't really room in the circle for ten. Have the children join hands and all move to the second circle, the one on the left. Then say to them, "We have ten ones but we also have one ten." This is the crux of the concept. If they understand this, they are well on their way. Then say, "To make it easier to work with big numbers we will make (Billy, Margy, or whomever) one ten. When Billy stands in the circle on the left, he is one ten. When he stands in the right circle, he is one one." Ask the other nine children to sit down. "Now Billy is one ten." *Crucial.* Erase the nine in the first square and place a *one* in the second square. Draw their attention to the fact that no one is standing in the first circle. Say "What we have is one ten and no ones." Then place a zero in the first square.

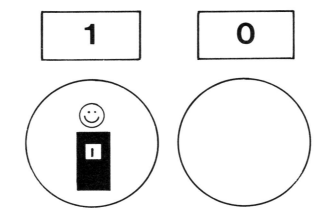

Lastly, have another child go up and stand in the first circle. Ask the children what they see now. One ten and one one. Change the zero in the first square to a one.

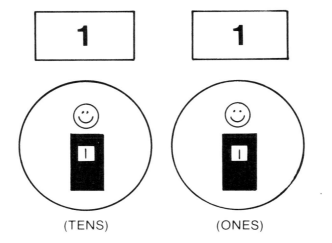

(TENS) (ONES)

"One ten and one one." Then ask the children if they know the name for the number with two ones side by side.
"Eleven."

Right, so we have one ten and one one, and we also call that eleven.

Note:

In other words, let them see it, by letting them be it. Stop at this point.

One could easily adapt this to the teaching of bases in 6th-7th grade. "Why be limited to groups of ten, why not groups of 6,7 etc . . .?"

Evaluation:

Children's understanding of the concept.

2. Left Mode

Analyze The Experience

Teacher More Active

Objective:

To allow the children to discuss/examine what happened.

Activity:

Talk about it and let the children *be* other numbers; i.e. two children stand in the second circle, one in the first, what number "21" is, and so on.

Evaluation:

Participation and level of understanding of the concept.

QUADRANT TWO

CONCEPT FORMULATION

THE ANALYTIC LEARNER'S MOST COMFORTABLE PLACE

CONCERN FOR THE FACTS AS EXPERTS SEE THEM — TEACH IT TO THEM

Answer the question "WHAT?"

Teacher's Role — Information Giver

Method — Informational

---

3. Right Mode

Integrate Reflections Into Concepts

Teacher More Active

Objective:

To switch the concept to practice in another medium.

Activity:

Give the children sticks (toothpicks etc.) and rubber bands. Let them manipulate the sticks in various combinations of tens and ones. i.e. numbers apply to anything, people, toothpicks, apples etc. Teacher gives problems, 22, 17, 31 etc.

Evaluation:

Do the children understand? Teacher can assist those who need more help.

---

4. Left Mode

Develop Theories And Concepts

Teacher More Active

Objective:

To teach place value concept through teacher instruction.

Activity:

Teacher teaches. Any good primary math text will provide assistance.

Evaluation:

Objective test.

QUADRANT THREE

PRACTICE AND PERSONALIZATION

THE COMMON SENSE LEARNER'S MOST COMFORTABLE PLACE

CONCERN FOR HANDS-ON EXPERIENCE — LET THEM TRY IT

Answer the question "HOW DOES THIS WORK?"

Teacher's Role — Coach/Facilitator

Method — Facilitation

---

5. Left Mode

Working On Defined Concepts

(Reinforcement and Manipulation)

Students More Active

Objective:

To give additional practice in the concept.

Activity:

Workbooks from any good primary math text.

Evaluation:

Quality and accuracy of above.

6. Right Mode

"Messing Around"

(Adding something of themselves)

Students More Active

Objective:

To introduce aural and kinetic practice methods (aural = listening; kinetic = use of body [tactile])

Activity:

Have the children *listen* to problems and write answers. Have the children use *tactile* approach to problems, i.e., sandpaper numbers with blindfolds on — three dimensional numbers which are combined into problems manipulated also with blindfolds on, etc.

Note:

Always attempt to use aural and kinetic methods in addition to the visual. Children vary in their preferences for these methods.

Evaluation:

Quality of their manipulations.

QUADRANT FOUR

*INTEGRATING APPLICATION
AND EXPERIENCE*

THE DYNAMIC LEARNER'S MOST
COMFORTABLE PLACE

CONCERN FOR ACTION, DOING — LET THEM
TEACH IT TO THEMSELVES AND SHARE
WHAT THEY LEARN WITH OTHERS

Answers the questions
"WHAT CAN THIS BECOME?"
"WHAT CAN I MAKE OF THIS?"

Teacher's Role — Evaluator/Remediator

Method — Self-Discovery

7. Left Mode

**Analyzing Their Own Application Of The
Concepts For Usefulness, Originality, And As A
Stepping Stone For Future Learning**

Students More Active

Objective:

To talk about making up problems of their own
to try on each other.

To make the learned material personal.

Activity:

Have the children make up worksheets to try on
each other. i.e. Fill in blanks ③ ④ = 3 10's
and 4 1's (and reverse). Now make toothpick
structures on all problems from work sheets.

Evaluation:

Quality of worksheets.

8. Right Mode

**Doing It Themselves And Sharing What They Do
With Others**

(Integrating Application and Experience)

Students More Active

Objective:

To share their learning.

Activity:

Children give worksheets to each other, do them
and correct (help) each other.

Evaluation:

Participation and sharing.

The Complete 4MAT System Model

Math Unit: Place Value   **Primary**

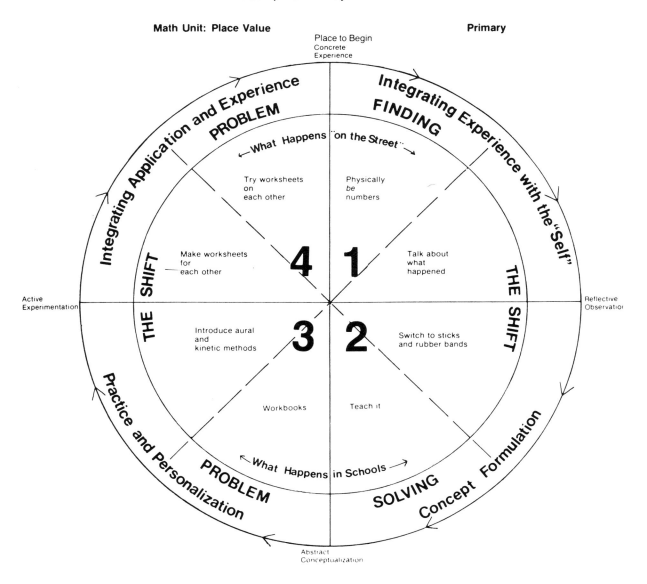

Place to Begin
Concrete
Experience

Integrating Application and Experience
PROBLEM

Integrating Experience with the "Self"
FINDING

← What Happens on the Street →

Try worksheets on each other

Physically *be* numbers

THE SHIFT

Make worksheets for each other

Talk about what happened

4 **1**

THE SHIFT

Active Experimentation

Reflective Observation

THE SHIFT

Introduce aural and kinetic methods

Switch to sticks and rubber bands

3 **2**

THE SHIFT

Workbooks

Teach it

Practice and Personalization
PROBLEM

← What Happens in Schools →

SOLVING

Concept Formulation

Abstract
Conceptualization

Subject: Science   Unit: Living and Non-living Things   Grade Level: Primary

AUTHOR: MARLENE WIECZOREK BOWEN

THEME: "Without a knowledge of science, one cannot understand current events."   J. B. S. Haldane

"Science is but the statement of truth found out."   Coley

QUADRANT ONE

INTEGRATING EXPERIENCE WITH THE SELF

THE IMAGINATIVE LEARNER'S MOST COMFORTABLE PLACE

CONCERN WITH PERSONAL MEANING — CREATE A REASON

Answer the question "WHY?"

Teacher's Role — Motivator

Method — Simulation to encourage brainstorming for imagination, innovation, and empathy

---

1. Right Mode

Create An Experience

Teacher More Active

Objective:

To enhance their experience of the difference between living and nonliving things.

Main idea: Living things eat, move, and grow.

Activity:

Children plant bean seeds. (Any good primary level science text will list materials and process.)

Introduce living animals to classroom for children to observe and enjoy. Discuss proper care.

Have the children collect and post pictures of living things.

Evaluation:

Quality of picture collections.

2. Left Mode

Analyze The Experience

Teacher More Active

Objective:

To help students understand that objects may be classified as living or nonliving things.

To learn to systematically observe changes in growth.

Activity:

Children collect stones, leaves, insects, weed, sea shells, twigs and seeds. Divide class into groups of four children. Children classify the objects into two groups: living and nonliving. Each group of four children labels its display.

Children keep a record of their bean seed planting:

I planted seeds on _____
I saw a stem on _____
I saw roots on _____
I saw leaves on _____

Children are given observation work sheets for their bean plants.

Observation sheets:
1. How does it grow?
2. How much water does it need? How can I tell?
3. How often do I have to turn it so it gets equal light? Why is that?

Children keep a growth record of what their plant looks like each day (for 6 days), drawing the progress.

Day 1	Day 2	Day 3

Day 4	Day 5	Day 6

Discuss growth of plants and other activities.

Evaluation:

Bean seed planting record, observation sheets, growth records.

QUADRANT TWO

CONCEPT FORMULATION

THE ANALYTIC LEARNER'S MOST COMFORTABLE PLACE

CONCERN FOR THE FACTS AS EXPERTS SEE THEM — TEACH IT TO THEM

Answer the question "WHAT?"

Teacher's Role — Information Giver

Method — Informational

---

3. Right Mode

Integrate Reflections Into Concepts

Teacher More Active

Objective:

To help children understand that living things grow and nonliving things do not.

Activity:

Have them bring in pictures of themselves as babies, post them. Collect pictures of:

a baby,	a young person of 18-19,
a child of 6-7,	a person about 40,
a child of 12-13,	a person of 60.

Evaluation:

Picture collection.

4. Left Mode

Develop Theories and Concepts

Teacher More Active

Objective:

To understand major elements needed for growth. To understand living things grow, eat and move.

Activity:

Teach lesson on plants taking food, animals needing food, etc. Any good science text will contain the information needed. Children also read from their science texts, review the properties of living things.

Evaluation:

Objective Test.

QUADRANT THREE

PRACTICE AND PERSONALIZATION

THE COMMON SENSE LEARNER'S MOST COMFORTABLE PLACE

CONCERN FOR HANDS-ON EXPERIENCE — LET THEM TRY IT

Answer the question "HOW DOES THIS WORK?"

Teacher's Role — Coach/Facilitator

Method — Facilitation

---

5. Left Mode

Working On Defined Concepts

(Reinforcement and Manipulation)

Students More Active

Objective:

To reinforce their understanding of growth and change in living and nonliving things.

Activity:

Worksheets, end of chapter questions, and activities from text.
Note: Excellent examples can be found in a new science series. D. C. Heath and Company.[4]

Evaluation:

Quality of worksheets, etc.

6. Right Mode

"Messing Around"

(Adding Something of Themselves)

Students More Active

Objective:

To personalize their learning in some meaningful, unique way.

Activity:

Children choose an activity with teacher's help and begin collecting materials.

Examples: Construct a mobile of living things. Construct a mobile of nonliving things. Do two sculptures in clay: one living, one nonliving. Write a poem about how living things grow. Do seed mosaics. Encourage them to use the materials they collected in Step Two.

Evaluation:

Completion of project

QUADRANT FOUR

*INTEGRATING APPLICATION
AND EXPERIENCE*

THE DYNAMIC LEARNER'S MOST
COMFORTABLE PLACE

CONCERN FOR ACTION, DOING — LET THEM
TEACH IT TO THEMSELVES AND SHARE
WHAT THEY LEARN WITH OTHERS

Answer the questions
"WHAT CAN THIS BECOME?"
"WHAT CAN I MAKE OF THIS?"

Teacher's Role — Evaluator/Remediator

Method — Self-Discovery

---

7. Left Mode

**Analyzing Their Own Application Of The
Concepts For Usefulness, Originality, And As A
Stepping Stone For Future Learning**

Students More Active

Objective:

To teach them how to systematize a project plan.

Activity:

Students fill in the data for the following form:

I am making a _____

I will need _____

It will show (lesson concept) _____

It will be finished on _____

Name _____

Teacher's Signature _____

Evaluation:

Project plan.

8. Right Mode

**Doing It Themselves And Sharing What They Do
With Others**

(Integrating Application and Experience)

Students More Active

Objective:

To follow through on a plan to personalize their
learning.

To share what they learn and do with others.

Activity:

Children complete their projects and display
them in the classroom. They explain them to
their classmates.

Evaluation:

Completion of project.

The Complete 4MAT System Model

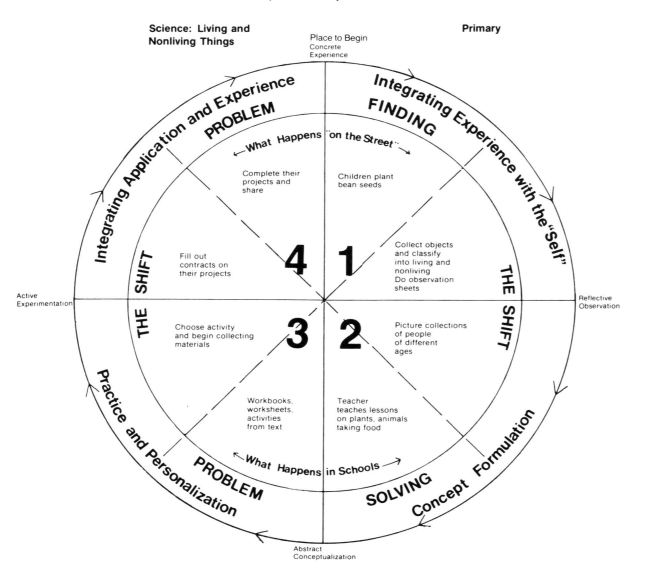

Science: Living and Nonliving Things

Primary

Place to Begin
Concrete Experience

Integrating Experience with the "Self"

Integrating Application and Experience

PROBLEM FINDING

What Happens "on the Street"

Complete their projects and share

Children plant bean seeds

THE SHIFT

Fill out contracts on their projects

4 **1**

Collect objects and classify into living and nonliving Do observation sheets

THE SHIFT

Active Experimentation

Reflective Observation

THE SHIFT

Choose activity and begin collecting materials

3 **2**

Picture collections of people of different ages

Workbooks, worksheets, activities from text

Teacher teaches lessons on plants, animals taking food

Practice and Personalization

PROBLEM SOLVING

What Happens in Schools

Concept Formulation

Abstract Conceptualization

Intermediate Units

Subject: Science   Unit: Insects   Grade Level: Intermediate

AUTHOR: MARLENE WIECZOREK BOWEN

THEME: "We live in a bountiful nature, filled with diversities and likenesses."
McCarthy

QUADRANT ONE

INTEGRATING EXPERIENCE WITH THE SELF

THE IMAGINATIVE LEARNER'S MOST COMFORTABLE PLACE

CONCERN WITH PERSONAL MEANING — CREATE A REASON

Answer the question "WHY?"

Teacher's Role — Motivator

Method — Simulation to encourage brainstorming for imagination, innovation, and empathy

---

1. Right Mode

Create An Experience

Teacher More Active

Objective:

To observe and experience a living insect.

To enhance observational skills.

Activity:

Students are assigned partners. Each pair of students is given its own live grasshopper.

Containers: *large* glass jar covered with screen and/or cheesecloth. Add leaves, grass, food and water. Place on shelf or counter that allows for sun and shade. Instruct students as to proper care. Give them the following observation worksheets.

1. Name the body parts (head, thorax, abdomen).
2. Sketch and label them.
3. Observe the antennae. Are they thick or thin?
4. Sketch the antennae. What do you think they are for?
5. How many legs? All the same length? Are there joints?
6. Sketch the legs.
7. Are there wings?
8. What does your grasshopper eat?
9. How does it eat? Suck, bite or chew?
10. What environment does your grasshopper need?
11. What is its range of activity? Does light or darkness affect its activity?
12. Name your grasshopper.
13. Both of you must make a sketch of your grasshopper. Refer to your textbook if you need help.

Evaluation:

Quality and accuracy of worksheets.

2. Left Mode

Analyze The Experience

Teacher More Active

Objective:

To pool observations and begin systematizing data.

Activity:

Discussion of work sheets and observations. (In the class in which we piloted this lesson, we collected the grasshoppers after two weeks and changed the containers, and to our amazement, the students were able to identify their own.)

Evaluation:

Quality of the discussion.

QUADRANT TWO

CONCEPT FORMULATION

THE ANALYTIC LEARNER'S MOST COMFORTABLE PLACE

CONCERN FOR THE FACTS AS EXPERTS SEE THEM — TEACH IT TO THEM

Answer the question "WHAT?"

Teacher's Role — Information Giver

Method — Informational

---

3. Right Mode

Integrate Reflections Into Concepts

Teacher More Active

Objective:

To provide an activity that will broaden their grasshopper experience to insects in general in preparation for lecture and reading materials.

Activity:

Instruct students to begin their own insect collections. Any good science text will explain this process.

Evaluation:

Insect collecting process.

4. Left Mode

Develop Theories And Concepts

Teacher More Active

Objective:

To teach stages of insect growth.

Activity:

Lecture with accompanying text; eggs, larvae, pupae, adults; eggs, nymphs, adults.
Read the assigned chapters in the text.

Evaluation:

Objective test.

QUADRANT THREE

PRACTICE AND PERSONALIZATION

THE COMMON SENSE LEARNER'S MOST COMFORTABLE PLACE

CONCERN FOR HANDS-ON EXPERIENCE — LET THEM TRY IT

Answer the question "HOW DOES THIS WORK?"

Teacher's Role — Coach/Facilitator

Method — Facilitation

---

5. Left Mode

Working On Defined Concepts

(Reinforcement and Manipulation)

Students More Active

Objective:

To practice the concepts and reinforce the learning.

Activity:

Workbooks, worksheets, activities in text.

Students begin identifying their insect collections.

Evaluation:

Quality and accuracy of the above.

6. Right Mode

"Messing Around"

(Adding Something of Themselves)

Students More Active

Objective:

To personalize students' learning by allowing them to choose an activity that explores some facet of insect life.

Activity:

Do a sketchbook of various insects. Do sculptures of various insects. (Teachers should use some of the excellent experiments listed in various science texts.)

**Invent and build an insect, using what you now know about insects.
(Have various materials:
pieces of styrofoam, toothpicks, remnants of cloth, colored paper, pipe cleaners, etc. Consider an all-school display.)**

Note:

The author has recently examined several new science texts and enthusiastically recommends the Heath Series, 1981, as an excellent example of right and left processing techniques.[5]

At this step the students turn in a project plan for teacher and (where necessary) parent approval. They write a contract specifying: the project, the materials needed, the resources, the concepts to be examined, worked through or tested, and the date of completion.

Evaluation:

How well the students go about the task of planning their projects and the scope of their activity.

QUADRANT FOUR

*INTEGRATING APPLICATION
AND EXPERIENCE*

THE DYNAMIC LEARNER'S MOST
COMFORTABLE PLACE

CONCERN FOR ACTION, DOING — LET THEM
TEACH IT TO THEMSELVES AND SHARE
WHAT THEY LEARN WITH OTHERS

Answer the questions
"WHAT CAN THIS BECOME?"
"WHAT CAN I MAKE OF THIS?"

Teacher's Role — Evaluator/Remediator

Method — Self-Discovery

---

7. Left Mode

Analyzing Their Own Application Of The Concepts For Usefulness, Originality, And As A Stepping Stone For Future Learning

Students More Active

Objective:

To enhance student ability to plan and work systematically.

Activity:

Students begin their projects.

Evaluation:

The manner in which they "get to work."

8. Right Mode

Doing It Themselves And Sharing What They Do With Others

(Integrating Application and Experience)

Students More Active

Objective:

To increase student ability to complete what they begin. To give them the opportunity to explain what they have learned.

Activity:

Students complete their contracted projects and present them to their classmates, either by display, explanation or both.

Evaluation:

Quality of completed projects, faithfulness to project contract and quality of sharing.

The Complete 4MAT System Model

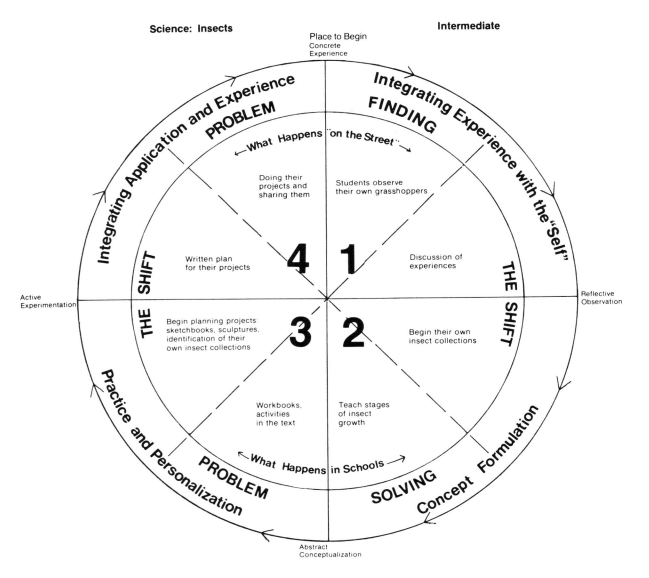

Science: Insects   Intermediate

Place to Begin
Concrete
Experience

Integrating Application and Experience
PROBLEM
FINDING
Integrating Experience with the "Self"

What Happens "on the Street"

Doing their projects and sharing them

Students observe their own grasshoppers

THE SHIFT

Written plan for their projects

4 **1**

Discussion of experiences

THE SHIFT

Active Experimentation

Reflective Observation

THE SHIFT

Begin planning projects: sketchbooks, sculptures, identification of their own insect collections

3 **2**

Begin their own insect collections

Practice and Personalization

Workbooks, activities in the text

Teach stages of insect growth

Concept Formulation

PROBLEM
SOLVING

What Happens in Schools

Abstract Conceptualization

AUTHORS: MARILYN AND PETER TANTILLO

THEME: "The study of mathematics gives grasp and power to the mind."
Tryon Edwards

QUADRANT ONE

INTEGRATING EXPERIENCE WITH THE SELF

THE IMAGINATIVE LEARNER'S MOST COMFORTABLE PLACE

CONCERN WITH PERSONAL MEANING — CREATE A REASON

Answer the question "WHY?"

Teacher's Role — Motivator

Method — Simulation to encourage brainstorming for imagination, innovation, and empathy

---

1. Right Mode

Create An Experience

Teacher More Active

Objective:

To create an experience of fractional equivalence and the need for a common denominator to combine fractional parts.

Activity:

Serve a special snack. You will need two identical rectangular pans of brownies. Cut one pan into four equal strips. Cut the other pan into five equal parts.

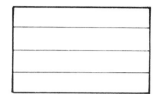 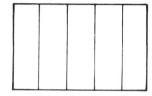

Show the students the two pans. Ask them to identify what fractional part is represented by the pieces of brownies in each pan. (1/4 and 1/5.) Ask them if they can think of a way to cut the brownies so that all the pieces from both pans are equal in size.

Then cut across the slices in each pan: four evenly spaced cuts across the 4/4 pan, three evenly spaced cuts across the 5/5 pan.

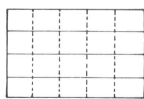 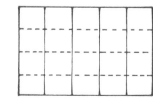

Ask if all the pieces are about the same size. (Yes, approximately.) Were the large pieces (strips) equal before they were cut? (No, 1/5 does not equal 1/4.) Then have the students identify the new fractional names for the brownies in each pan. (4/4=20/20 and 5/5=20/20.) Ask the students how many pieces we have all together. (40 pieces, each piece 1/20 of its pan, 2 pans, therefore 40/20ths.) Then distribute the brownies to the students.

Evaluation:

Quality of discussion and understanding of what was done.

2. Left Mode

Analyze The Experience

Teacher More Active

Objective:

To discuss the renaming of fractions.

Activity:

After the snack and cleanup discuss the following questions: How much cake was in each pan? (One whole cake.) How much cake did we have in both pans? (Two wholes.) Was there more/less/same amount of cake after it was cut? (same.) Could the cake have been cut into more pieces? (Yes.) Would the total amount have been different? (No.) When the pans were first brought in, were the pieces equal? Were there enough pieces to go around? (No.) How did we end up with 20 pieces in each pan when we started with 4 and 5 in each pan? Were we able to make the large strips into equal pieces? How?

Evaluation:

Quality of the discussion and answers.

QUADRANT TWO

CONCEPT FORMULATION

THE ANALYTIC LEARNER'S MOST
COMFORTABLE PLACE

CONCERN FOR THE FACTS AS EXPERTS SEE
THEM — TEACH IT TO THEM

Answer the question "WHAT?"

Teacher's Role — Information Giver

Method — Informational

---

3. Right Mode

Integrate Reflections Into Concepts

Teacher More Active.

Objective:

To formulate the concepts of fractional equivalence and renaming fractions through another medium.

Activity:

Divide the class into groups of three or four. Each group will need pairs of scissors, six sheets of construction paper in six different colors, and one question sheet. (See below.) Instruct the groups to divide up the tasks. Each group must fold, then cut the construction paper in the following way:

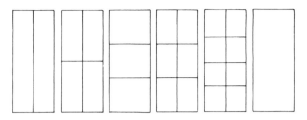

yellow   green   red   orange   blue   black

Yellow is folded/cut into two equal pieces.
Green is folded/cut into four equal pieces.
Red is folded/cut into three equal pieces. (Fold like a letter.)
Orange is folded/cut into six equal pieces.
Blue is folded/cut into eight equal pieces.
Black is left whole.

On each yellow piece write 1/2
On each green piece write 1/4
On each red piece write 1/3
On each orange piece write 1/6
On each blue piece write 1/8
In chalk on the black piece write 1 = 1/1

Each group prepares the pieces, then uses them to answer the questions on the question sheet.

Fractions activity question sheet

GROUP NUMBER _____

How many pieces do you have of each color?

Yellow   _____
Green   _____
Red   _____
Orange   _____
Blue   _____
Black   _____

Can you make an arrangement the same size as a blue piece with any other color?

Can you make an arrangement the same size as a yellow piece with any other color?

How many blues does it take
to make one yellow?   _____
How many greens does it take
to make one yellow?   _____
How many oranges does it take
to make one yellow?   _____
How many blues does it take
to make one green?   _____
How many oranges does it take
to make one red?   _____
Can green pieces be used to make an arrangement the same size as one red piece?

Can orange pieces be used to make an arrangement the same size as one green piece?

How many yellows does it take
to make one black (a whole)? _____
How many greens does it take
to make one black (a whole)? _____
How many reds does it take
to make one black (a whole)? _____
How many oranges does it take
to make one black (a whole)? _____
How many blues does it take
to make one black (a whole)? _____

When each group has completed the assignment, the teacher leads a sharing session where the questions and answers are reviewed. Volunteers can be chosen to demonstrate their answers by comparing arrangements of pieces on the overhead projector. The teacher should stress these points in the sharing session: A whole can be divided into equal fractional parts in many different ways. In this division process, all pieces must be equal. Each piece's size can be represented by a fraction. Some pieces (fractions) can be duplicated by arrangements of sets of smaller pieces. Therefore, some fractions are equivalent to fractions with different denominators.

After the sharing session, the teacher should write pairs of equivalent fractions which the students know on the board. S/he can then follow up with an explanation of changing a fraction into an equivalent by multiplying both the numerator and denominator by the same number.

Evaluation:

Group participation and comprehension of concepts.

4. Left Mode

Develop Theories And Concepts

Teacher More Active

Objective:

To explain the concepts of: least common multiple, equivalent fractions, adding fractions with like denominators, subtracting fractions with like denominators, adding fractions with different denominators, subtracting fractions with different denominators.

Activity:

Lecture and illustrate sample problems on the blackboard. Any good intermediate math text will assist.

Evaluation:

Objective test.

QUADRANT THREE

PRACTICE AND PERSONALIZATION

THE COMMON SENSE LEARNER'S MOST COMFORTABLE PLACE

CONCERN FOR HANDS-ON EXPERIENCE — LET THEM TRY IT

Answer the question "HOW DOES THIS WORK?"

Teacher's Role — Coach/Facilitator

Method — Facilitation

5. Left Mode

Working On Defined Concepts

(Reinforcement and Manipulation)

Students More Active

Objective:

To reinforce the taught concepts.

Activity:

Workbooks, worksheets, problems from text.

Evaluation:

Quality and accuracy of the above.

6. Right Mode

"Messing Around"

(Adding Something of Themselves)

Students More Active

Objective:

To allow students to make and play a game which will reinforce the taught concepts.

Activity:

The game is a variation of Bingo. The teacher takes recently worked on problems and copies them onto index cards which will be drawn from a box. The teacher then puts the *answers* to the problems on the index cards on the blackboard. Each student makes his or her own game card in the following way:

On a sheet of paper make a grid of sixteen boxes, that is, four rows and four columns. In each box the students write a fraction from the list which is written on the blackboard. The problem/answer list should include thirty to forty different answers from which the students will select their sixteen choices for their boxes. Students should be encouraged to select the numbers randomly from the entire list so that no two game cards will be alike. The teacher draws a problem card from the box and lists it on the board or calls it out. Students determine the answer to the problem, they check their game card to see if the answer was one they had placed on their card. (If the class is not yet skilled enough to determine the answers on their own or if there are several students who would benefit, ask volunteers to come up to the board and work out the problem. In this way, slower students are not eliminated from play, but rather are shown sample problems for reinforcement of the procedure.) Play continues until one student has circled four answers in any row, column or diagonal, or all sixteen spaces as time allows. Teacher should determine prizes or incentives before play begins.

Evaluation:

Students' enjoyment and accuracy.

QUADRANT FOUR

INTEGRATING APPLICATION AND EXPERIENCE

THE DYNAMIC LEARNER'S MOST COMFORTABLE PLACE

CONCERN FOR ACTION, DOING — LET THEM TEACH IT TO THEMSELVES AND SHARE WHAT THEY LEARN WITH OTHERS

Answer the questions
"WHAT CAN THIS BECOME?"
"WHAT CAN I MAKE OF THIS?"

Teacher's Role — Evaluator/Remediator

Method — Self-Discovery

7. Left Mode

Analyzing Their Own Application Of The Concepts For Usefulness, Originality, And As A Stepping Stone For Future Learning

Students More Active

Objective:

To make up word problems.

Activity:

The teacher recalls sample problems from worksheets, workbooks, and text. The students are then asked to find their own examples of how fractions are used in everyday life.

Examples: using rulers to measure lengths, buying cloth, lumber, etc., measuring liquids for recipes, buying food by the pound, figuring postage by weight.

The students are then asked to make up several word problems. Each problem should be written out completely and solved with all the work shown.

Evaluation:

Appropriateness of examples and accuracy of solutions.

8. Right Mode

Doing It Themselves And Sharing What They Do With Others

(Integrating Application and Experience)

Students More Active

Objective:

To share the applications and uses of fractions with other students.

To give further practice in fractions.

Activity:

Students pair up to present their problems to one another. Students quiz one another with the problems.

Evaluation:

Participation and quality of their answers. Students can participate in evaluating each other.

The Complete 4MAT System Model

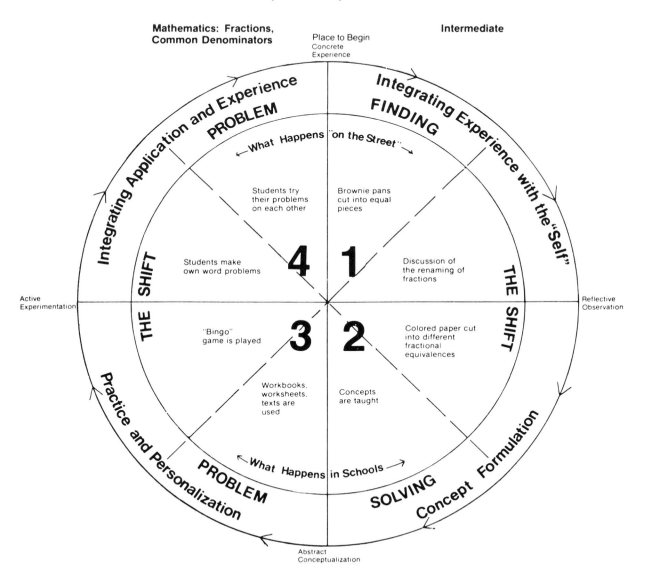

Mathematics: Fractions, Common Denominators

Intermediate

Place to Begin
Concrete Experience

Integrating Experience with the "Self"

Integrating Application and Experience

PROBLEM FINDING

←What Happens "on the Street"→

Students try their problems on each other

Brownie pans cut into equal pieces

Students make own word problems

4 **1**

Discussion of the renaming of fractions

THE SHIFT

THE SHIFT

Active Experimentation

Reflective Observation

"Bingo" game is played

3 **2**

Colored paper cut into different fractional equivalences

Workbooks, worksheets, texts are used

Concepts are taught

Practice and Personalization

PROBLEM ←What Happens in Schools→ SOLVING

Concept Formulation

Abstract Conceptualization

AUTHOR: ROBBIN LYNNE DAIGLE

THEME: "There is no feeling, except the extremes of fear and grief, that does not find relief in music."

George Eliot

"It is in learning music that many youthful hearts learn to love."

Ricard

QUADRANT ONE

INTEGRATING EXPERIENCE WITH THE SELF

THE IMAGINATIVE LEARNER'S MOST COMFORTABLE PLACE

CONCERN WITH PERSONAL MEANING — CREATE A REASON

Answer the question "WHY?"

Teacher's Role — Motivator

Method — Simulation to encourage brainstorming for imagination, innovation, and empathy

---

1. Right Mode

Create An Experience

Teacher More Active

Objective:

To help students experience note value (counts) with their bodies (4/4 meter, 4 beats in a measure, and a quarter note gets one count.)

Activity:

Use of aural and kinetic senses.

1. Students stand at their desks.
2. Teacher shows each of the following icons (graphic displays).

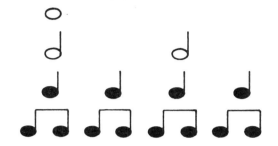

Teacher shows each of these icons, one at a time, while demonstrating the body movements for each.[6]

Tra-a-a-ain

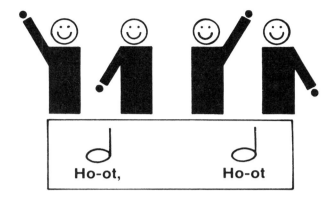

Ho-ot,   **Ho-ot**

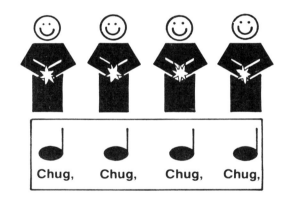

Chug,   Chug,   Chug,   Chug,

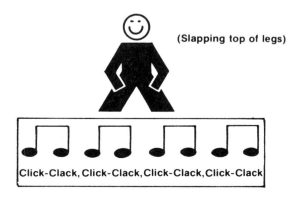

(Slapping top of legs)

Click-Clack, Click-Clack, Click-Clack, Click-Clack

3.* Teacher keeps steady beat with hand drum while calling out the icons for all children to do.

4. Have the class remain standing. Divide the children into two sections.

5. Assign group one a note value. Assign group two a different note value.

6. Bring the groups in one at a time with the hand drum keeping a steady beat.

7. When both groups are going, give one group a new note value.

8. After they are established again, give the second group a new note value.

9. Now divide the class into three sections and repeat the above procedure.

*When I read this lesson plan, I realized Robbin had asked the children to do a "bi-cognitive" task; a task requiring simultaneous processing in both left and right modes. There is evidence that requiring bi-cognitive tasks increases bi-cognitive functioning. See Ned Herrmann, *General Electric Whole Brained Seminars*.[7]

10. When the three sections have been mastered, divide the class into four parts.

The group in the first section = whole notes
The group in the second section = half notes
The group in the third section = quarter notes
The group in the fourth section = eighth notes

11. Begin with group one, bringing in groups two, three, and four one at a time.

12. After they master this, have students switch to the note value of the group to their left. Whole notes switch to half notes
Half notes switch to quarter notes

Quarter notes switch to eighth notes
Eighth notes switch to whole notes

13. Switch until groups return to original parts.

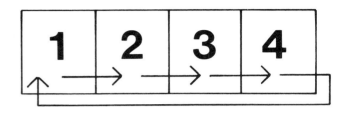

This is a difficult concept. It must be approached in the above progression in order to succeed.

Evaluation:

Ability of the groups to master the switching.

2. Left Mode

Analyze The Experience

Teacher More Active

Objective:

To examine the experience just completed.

Activity:

Lead the group in a discussion of the following questions:

How many counts did you feel for one saying of "Train"? (4) How many of those counts did you feel an accent on? (1) In the same space of time, how many "hoots" did you say? (2) How many accents did you feel then? (2) Was this an easy or difficult pattern for you to do? (This is the hardest pattern to feel, the one the students get mixed up the most.) What kind of beat did you hear from the drum when you said "Chug Chug"? (Steady beat.) What kind of beat did "Chug Chug" keep *in relation to the other patterns?* (The same beat.) If you said "Click Clack Click Clack Click Clack Click Clack," how many times did you patsch (slap your legs)? (8) Which was the slowest pattern? Which was the fastest pattern? Which pattern kept the steady beat?

Evaluation:

Quality of children's answers.

QUADRANT TWO

CONCEPT FORMULATION

THE ANALYTIC LEARNER'S MOST COMFORTABLE PLACE

CONCERN FOR THE FACTS AS EXPERTS SEE THEM — TEACH IT TO THEM

Answer the question "WHAT?"

Teacher's Role — Information Giver

Method — Informational

3. Right Mode

Integrate Reflections Into Concepts

Teacher More Active

Objective:

To deal with the subdivision of note value metaphorically.

Activity:

"Maisy the Daisy" Graphic Display

Maisy is a daisy in the wind.
The wind gusts hit her in sets of four.
(Whoosh, whoosh, whoosh, whoosh.)

Let's clap once for Maisy,
and then once for each petal Maisy
loses when the wind blows.

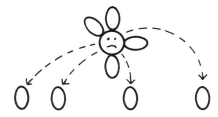

The longer Maisy is in the wind,
the more petals she loses.

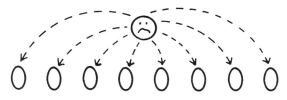

Do you see how the whole daisy
breaks down into eight smaller petals?

Do you also see how those eight smaller petals
together equal the whole daisy?

Evaluation:

Quality of children's responses.

4. Left Mode

Develop Theories And Concepts

Teacher More Active

Objective:

To reteach and reinforce the basic concepts.

Activity:

Explanation of meter signature. "The top number tells you how many counts there are in a measure, and the bottom number tells you what kind of note gets one count."
Note review: whole note = whole measure, etc.

Using felt board return to basic concepts. Put note value symbols in combinations of notes on felt board. "How many counts have I put in this measure? How many should be there?" "What kinds of notes could you use to fill in the missing counts?" Have children come up and put symbols on the board.

Felt Board

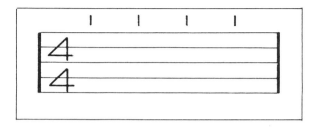

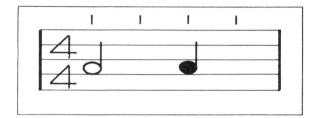

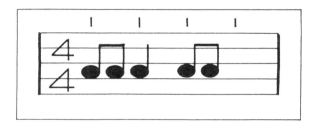

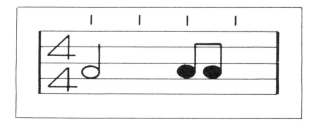

Evaluation:

Quality and accuracy of children's responses.

166

QUADRANT THREE

PRACTICE AND PERSONALIZATION

THE COMMON SENSE LEARNER'S MOST COMFORTABLE PLACE

CONCERN FOR HANDS-ON EXPERIENCE — LET THEM TRY IT

Answer the question "HOW DOES THIS WORK?"

Teacher's Role — Coach/Facilitator

Method — Facilitation

---

5. Left Mode

Working On Defined Concepts

(Reinforcement and Manipulation)

Students More Active

Objective:

To practice the concepts.

Activity:

Teacher beats out various combinations by clapping. Children write the patterns down in musical notation on music graph paper.

Various worksheets: For example, some combining fractions and note values.

Directions: Fill in the blanks with notes of proper value by figuring out what the sum of the problem is in 4/4 meter.

Figure by using mathematics, answer by using musical notes.

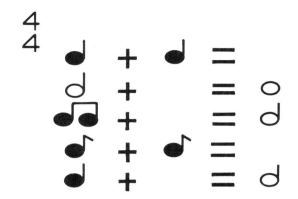

Later worksheets could deal with other meters, and more complex notation. i.e.,

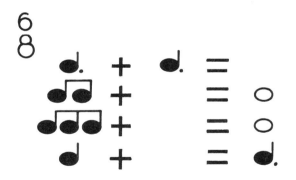

Many good music texts contain additional exercises for this concept.

Students must constantly keep in mind how many beats in a measure, and what kind of note gets one count.

Evaluation:

Quality and accuracy of worksheets.

6. Right Mode

"Messing Around"

(Adding Something of Themselves)

Students More Active

Objective:

To make their own meter compositions using the taught concepts.

Activity:

Put the children into groups of four. Have them create their own texts (related word series) to fit the previously given rhythms.

Evaluation:

Quality of texts.

QUADRANT FOUR

INTEGRATING APPLICATION AND EXPERIENCE

THE DYNAMIC LEARNER'S MOST COMFORTABLE PLACE

CONCERN FOR ACTION, DOING — LET THEM TEACH IT TO THEMSELVES AND SHARE WHAT THEY LEARN WITH OTHERS

Answer the questions
"WHAT CAN THIS BECOME?"
"WHAT CAN I MAKE OF THIS?"

Teacher's Role — Evaluator/Remediator

Method — Self-Discovery

---

7. Left Mode

Analyzing Their Own Application Of The Concepts For Usefulness, Originality, And As A Stepping Stone For Future Learning

Students More Active

Objective:

To transfer their own rhythm texts into musical notation.

To compose their own eight measure rhythmic composition.

Activity:

Students are asked to write their own rhythmic compositions using 4/4 meter, and whole, half, quarter, and eighth notes.

Additional activities (optional):
Write lyrics. Do art pictures of chant meanings or art depictions of text/beat feeling.

Evaluation:

Teacher checks to see if proper counts are in each measure.

8. Right Mode

Doing It Themselves And Sharing What They Have Done With Others

(Integrating Application and Experience)

Students More Active

Objective:

To share their own meter compositions with each other.

To get additional practice in the concepts.

Activity:

Children break into groups of four. They pass their compositions to the child on their right. Each gets a turn to clap out (better if one drum is available to each group of four) the compositions. Keep rotating until all compositions have been done.

Evaluation:

Participation and cooperation.

Note: Possibilities for next lessons(s): Teacher reviews student compositions, chooses one or two which will work particularly well, select students to be "performers."

Move on to more complicated notation, or introduce melodic concepts which may be applied to their previous rhythmic compositions. This is a perfect lead into a spiral on composing melodies and lyrics combining poetry with music.

The Complete 4MAT System Model

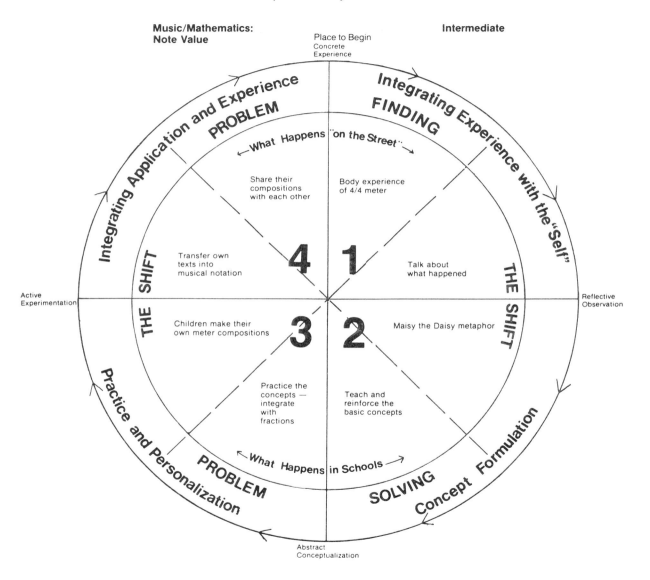

Music/Mathematics:
Note Value

Intermediate

Place to Begin
Concrete
Experience

Integrating Application and Experience

PROBLEM

Integrating Experience with the "Self"

FINDING

← What Happens "on the Street" →

Share their
compositions
with each other

Body experience
of 4/4 meter

4 **1**

THE SHIFT

Transfer own
texts into
musical notation

Talk about
what happened

THE SHIFT

Active
Experimentation

Reflective
Observation

THE SHIFT

Children make their
own meter compositions

3 **2**

Maisy the Daisy metaphor

Practice the
concepts —
integrate
with
fractions

Teach and
reinforce the
basic concepts

Practice and Personalization

PROBLEM

← What Happens in Schools →

SOLVING

Concept Formulation

Abstract
Conceptualization

Subject:
Physical Education and Art

Unit:
Line and Design

Grade Level:
Intermediate

AUTHOR: JOHN P. BENNETT

Commentary

The physical component of development is as important as intellectual and emotional development. It enhances or jeopardizes growth. The role of movement in one's ability to get along in society cannot be underestimated. How one moves is influenced by what one perceives. We perceive through all of our sensory mechanisms (sight, hearing, touch, smell, taste, feel). Children must be given the opportunity to explore and experiment with movement using all of their sensory mechanisms in a stimulating environment. Environments must be structured to appeal to as many different learning styles as is feasible. We need a variety of techniques in order to make the most of our students' abilities.

Our goal as teachers should be to develop the whole brains of our students. They arrive in school with a strong right brain orientation and we force them to switch almost totally to left brain processing. It is time we put the whole brain and the whole body to use. Physical expression, when it is allowed to be original with the individual, is a powerful means of engaging the whole brains of our students. The 4Mat System is designed to facilitate whole brain development.

QUADRANT ONE

INTEGRATING EXPERIENCE WITH THE SELF

THE IMAGINATIVE LEARNER'S MOST COMFORTABLE PLACE

CONCERN WITH PERSONAL MEANING — CREATE A REASON

Answer the question "WHY?"

Teacher's Role — Motivator

Method — Simulation to encourage brainstorming for imagination, innovation, and empathy

---

1. Right Mode

Create An Experience

Teacher More Active

Objective:

To create line and design through physical experience.

Activity:

(Need magic markers and construction paper) One child is asked to walk across the room in a straight line. The other children are asked to draw a representation of the line they saw. Another is asked to walk across the room in a jagged line. Again the children draw what they see. Repeat with a variety of lines. Then ask the children to draw

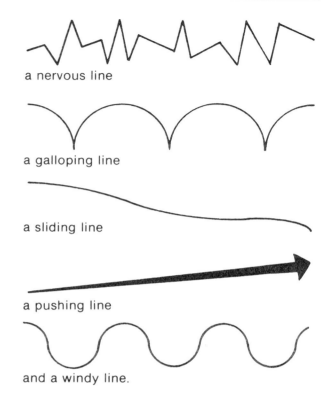

a nervous line

a galloping line

a sliding line

a pushing line

and a windy line.

2. Left Mode

Analyze The Experience

Teacher More Active

Objective:

To enhance the children's ability to examine experience.

Activity:

Discussion of what happened.

Was it hard to draw the lines you saw when Tom and Mary moved across the room?

What is a line?

QUADRANT TWO

CONCEPT FORMULATION

THE ANALYTIC LEARNER'S MOST COMFORTABLE PLACE

CONCERN FOR THE FACTS AS EXPERTS SEE THEM — TEACH IT TO THEM

Answer the question "WHAT?"

Teacher's Role — Information Giver

Method — Informational

---

3. Right Mode

Integrate Reflections Into Concepts

Teacher More Active

Objective:

To add to the student's understanding of the concept of line and movement.

Activity:

Ask the children to do the following with their bodies:
Can you show how a snowflake would move in a soft, gentle snow?
Now show me a hard, blowing snow!

Can you show how a marshmallow would melt in a cup of hot chocolate?

In groups of four, can you show me how a plant would sprout and grow in springtime?

Can you show how a drop of rain falls from the sky and hits the ground in a light rain?
In a heavy rain?

Can you walk this shape?

Do it another way.

Can you show me how a cricket would move if s/he had the hiccups?

Show me how a ping pong ball bounces.

Show me how a ship would sail on a calm day. How would it sail on a stormy day?

Can you do a movement sequence to this pattern?

4. Left Mode

Develop Theories And Concepts

Teacher More Active

Objective:

To develop the concept of movement in line.

Activity:

Teacher explains:

Lines and movements create shapes. When lines are put together they create shapes. Lines can create things we recognize that are found all around us.

Vocabulary: creative
imagine
design
line
nervous
jagged
sliding
pushing
windy

QUADRANT THREE

PRACTICE AND PERSONALIZATION

THE COMMON SENSE LEARNER'S MOST COMFORTABLE PLACE

CONCERN FOR HANDS-ON EXPERIENCE — LET THEM TRY IT

Answer the question "HOW DOES THIS WORK?"

Teacher's Role — Coach/Facilitator

Method — Facilitation

5. Left Mode

Working On Defined Concepts

(Reinforcement and Manipulation)

Students More Active

Objective:

To give practice in creating shapes from lines.

Activity:

Have some of the children form rectangles, then circles, then triangles, then squares with their bodies. Have the other children draw the shapes they see. Exchange places: doers and drawers.

6. Right Mode

"Messing Around"

(Adding Something of Themselves)

Students More Active

Objective:

To combine lines and shapes and emphasize contrasts.

Activity:

Have the children combine two shapes to make something new. Tell them the new shape must look "heavy."

Repeat the exercise, except this time the new shape must look "light and fluffy."

Repeat the exercise, except this time the new shape must look "sharp and jagged."

Repeat one more time, except this time the new shape must look "smooth."

QUADRANT FOUR

INTEGRATING APPLICATION AND EXPERIENCE

THE DYNAMIC LEARNER'S MOST COMFORTABLE PLACE

CONCERN FOR ACTION, DOING — LET THEM TEACH IT TO THEMSELVES AND SHARE WHAT THEY LEARN WITH OTHERS

Answer the questions
"WHAT CAN THIS BECOME?"
"WHAT CAN I MAKE OF THIS?"

Teacher's Role — Evaluator/Remediator

Method — Self-Discovery

7. Left Mode

Analyzing Their Own Application Of The Concepts For Usefulness, Originality, And As A Stepping Stone For Future Learning

Students More Active

Objective:

To plan and complete an art activity. To form shapes from lines.

Activity:

Ask the children to select several colors of paper. Then ask them to cut lines of different types and widths. Have them arrange their lines on a large piece of paper and paste them on. Remind them that the arrangements of their lines will create shapes on their papers.

8. Right Mode

Doing It Themselves And Sharing What They Do With Others

(Integrating Application and Experience)

Students More Active

Objective:

To add movement to shape.

To translate movement on a two-dimensional surface to their own bodies.

Activity:

Now have the children paint people or lines on their papers. People who are moving through, under, over, or into the shapes they have already created.

Pick some of the simpler ones when the children have finished and ask them to interpret through movement the content of the pictures.

Evaluation: (The only evaluation in all eight steps.)

The enjoyment of the children. Free them from worrying about the product. Let them enjoy the process and product will improve. Promote exploration, expansion, excelling.

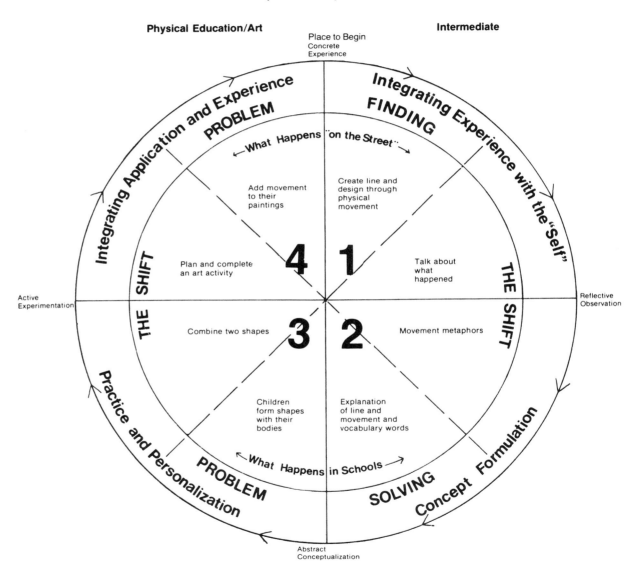

The Complete 4MAT System Model

Middle School Units

AUTHOR: BERNICE McCARTHY

THEME: "If the riches of the Indies, or the crowns of all the Kingdoms of Europe were laid at my feet in exchange for my love of reading, I would spurn them all."   Fenelon

"The love of reading enables a person to exchange the wearisome hours of life, which come to everyone, for hours of delight."

Montesquieu

QUADRANT ONE

INTEGRATING EXPERIENCE WITH THE SELF

THE IMAGINATIVE LEARNER'S MOST COMFORTABLE PLACE

CONCERN WITH PERSONAL MEANING — CREATE A REASON

Answer the question "WHY?"

Teacher's Role — Motivator

Method — Simulation to encourage brainstorming for imagination, innovation, and empathy

---

1. Right Mode

Create An Experience

Teacher More Active

Objective:

To help students truly understand the importance of reading.

Activity:

Divide students into groups of four. Give them the following worksheet.

Worksheet

You must do the following in a single day. Decide in your group how you would do these things.

Get on the right bus in an unfamiliar city.

Fill out a job application form.

Eat lunch in a fancy restaurant with the person who is interviewing you for a job you really need.

Assemble a complicated bike for your younger brother.

Understand a letter you receive from a very close friend.

Find out what happened to your favorite team when your TV set is broken.

Get a prescription at the drug store and take the proper amount of medicine.

There's one problem — YOU CANNOT READ!

Evaluation:

Group participation and responsibility of group members for getting the task accomplished.

---

2. Left Mode

Analyze The Experience

Teacher More Active

Objective:

To draw a composite picture of a nonreader in order to discuss the implications in today's world.

Activity:

Group reports on how a person would accomplish the tasks listed on the work sheet. Teacher lists problems faced on the board and guides the group into a composite of a nonreader: alternative methods of learning, frustration, lack of personal privacy in reading personal messages, embarrassment.

Lead into discussion of implications of non-reading for: financial success, time spent alone, adequate communication skills, learning the combined wisdom of great men/women of the past and present. Are TV, films and verbal communication skills adequate?

Evaluation:

Quality of discussion. Were the students engaged? Number of ideas generated.

QUADRANT TWO

CONCEPT FORMULATION

THE ANALYTIC LEARNER'S MOST
COMFORTABLE PLACE

CONCERN FOR THE FACTS AS EXPERTS SEE
THEM — TEACH IT TO THEM

Answer the question "WHAT?"

Teacher's Role — Information Giver

Method — Informational

---

3. Right Mode

Integrate Reflections Into Concepts

Teacher More Active

Objective:

To enhance their ability to read a story for
enjoyment and the main idea.

Activity:

Choose an exciting story with high interest and
have students read it in class (four to six pages.)

Have the students write what they feel are the
main relationships in the story. Have the students
write how they would feel if they were the main
character in the story.

Evaluation:

Quality of written work.

4. Left Mode

Develop Theories And Concepts

Teacher More Active

Objective:

To enhance their understanding of sequence of
events in a story.

To enlarge their vocabularies.

Activity:

Teacher does a chronological sequence of
events in the story, and develops a time line on
the board.

Teacher instructs as to specific meanings of new
vocabulary words, using root meanings.

Evaluation:

Objective test for chronological sequence of a
new story and vocabulary.

QUADRANT THREE

PRACTICE AND PERSONALIZATION

THE COMMON SENSE LEARNER'S MOST
COMFORTABLE PLACE

CONCERN FOR HANDS-ON EXPERIENCE —
LET THEM TRY IT

Answer the question "HOW DOES THIS WORK?"

Teacher's Role — Coach/Facilitator

Method — Facilitation

---

5. Left Mode

Working On Defined Concepts

(Reinforcement and Manipulation)

Students More Active

Objective:

To give practice in: outlining, listing details and
facts, drawing conclusions, and finding specific
dictionary meanings for new vocabulary words.

Activity:

Worksheets for the above.

Evaluation:

Quality of worksheets.

6. Right Mode

"Messing Around"

(Adding Something of Themselves)

Students More Active

Objective:

To put themselves into the story.

To enhance their understanding of the overall
unity of the story.

To gain practice in understanding emotional
connotations of words.

Activity:

Worksheets on: Anticipating the outcome of the story. (Where were the clues that helped you to guess the end of the story? Foreshadowings?) Unity of the flow of events. (How did the events make up a unified theme?) List the vocabulary words that seem to be the most heavily laden with emotional overtones (positive and negative words).

Finally, have the students put themselves into the story. Have them write a short essay on "What you would have done and said if you could have 'jumped into the story' at some point."

Evaluation:

Quality of the above with emphasis on imagination.

QUADRANT FOUR

INTEGRATING APPLICATION AND EXPERIENCE

THE DYNAMIC LEARNER'S MOST COMFORTABLE PLACE

CONCERN FOR ACTION, DOING — LET THEM TEACH IT TO THEMSELVES AND SHARE WHAT THEY LEARN WITH OTHERS

Answer the questions
"WHAT CAN THIS BECOME?"
"WHAT CAN I MAKE OF THIS?"

Teacher's Role — Evaluator/Remediator

Method — Self-Discovery

7. Left Mode

Analyzing Their Own Application Of The Concepts For Usefulness, Originality, And As A Stepping Stone For Future Learning

Students More Active

Objective:

To improve students' comprehension skills by giving them additional practice.

Activity:

Give the students brief written descriptions of four additional stories:

one on sports
one on romance
one adventure
one fantasy.

Students choose one to read themselves and do the following:

List the main idea and the details and facts. Write the author's description of the main character and your description based on how you would feel if you were that character. List the chronological sequence and describe the unity of the whole story.

Evaluation:

Quality of worksheets.

8. Right Mode

Doing It Themselves And Sharing What They Do With Others

(Integrating Application and Experience)

Students More Active

Objective:

To enhance their imagination.

Activity:

Students rewrite the ending of one of the stories.
Students depict one of the following graphically (without words)
Draw the main character, or sculpt the main character or show the sequence of events in the story with symbols and arrows in a flow chart form or do an abstract art form of the main conflict in the story.

Evaluation:

Quality of rewritten ending and art work.

LEFT AND RIGHT MODE READING COMPREHENSION ACTIVITIES

LEFT MODE

Rapid reading for specific information
Details and facts
Seeing the parts
Understanding the character as the author presents him/her
Understanding specific denotative meanings of vocabulary
Asking objective questions (the answers can be found in the text)
Grasping directly stated meanings
Drawing conclusions
Grasping sequence of ideas, events, or steps

RIGHT MODE

Rapid reading for background information
The main idea
Seeing the relationships, the patterns
Being the character, empathizing
Understanding emotional connotative meanings of vocabulary
Asking subjective questions (the answers are open-ended and based on one's life experiences)
Grasping implied meanings or drawing inferences
Anticipating outcomes
Grasping the unity of the flow

The Complete 4MAT System Model

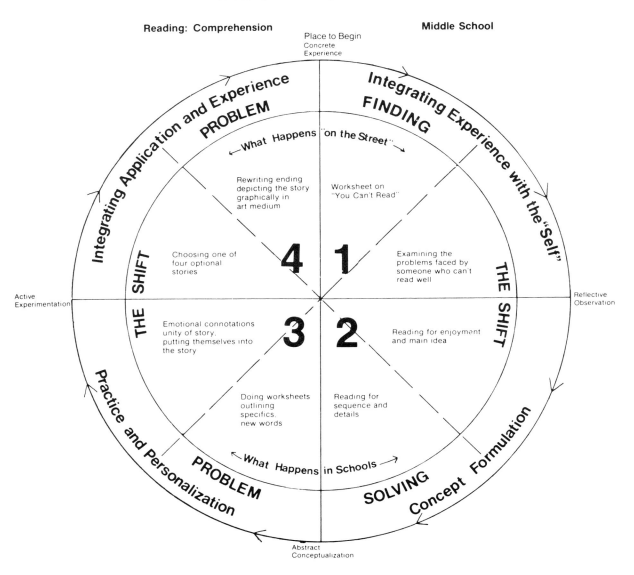

Reading: Comprehension

Middle School

Place to Begin
Concrete
Experience

Integrating Application and Experience
PROBLEM

Integrating Experience with the "Self"

FINDING

← What Happens "on the Street" →

Rewriting ending depicting the story graphically in art medium

Worksheet on "You Can't Read"

THE SHIFT

4 **1**

Choosing one of four optional stories

Examining the problems faced by someone who can't read well

THE SHIFT

Active
Experimentation

Reflective
Observation

Emotional connotations unity of story, putting themselves into the story

3 **2**

Reading for enjoyment and main idea

THE SHIFT

Doing worksheets outlining specifics, new words

Reading for sequence and details

Practice and Personalization

PROBLEM

← What Happens in Schools →

SOLVING

Concept Formulation

Abstract
Conceptualization

Subject: Mathematics   Unit: Probability   Grade Level: Middle School

AUTHORS: MARILYN AND PETER TANTILLO

THEME: "Probability: the relative frequency with which an event occurs or is likely to occur."

Random House Dictionary

QUADRANT ONE

INTEGRATING EXPERIENCE WITH THE SELF

THE IMAGINATIVE LEARNER'S MOST COMFORTABLE PLACE

CONCERN WITH PERSONAL MEANING — CREATE A REASON

Answer the question "WHY?"

Teacher's Role — Motivator

Method — Simulation to encourage brainstorming for imagination, innovation, and empathy

---

1. Right Mode

Create An Experience

Teacher More Active

Objective:

To provide the students with a personal experience of chance.

Activity:

Students test their own extra-sensory perception. Students use index cards to make decks of test cards using the standard testing symbols for ESP: square, circle, star, cross, wavy lines.

Each deck should contain twenty-five cards, five of each symbol. In groups of three, one student draws a card from the deck, and concentrates on the symbol. One student draws a card from the deck, and concentrates on the symbol. The second student, who is the test subject for this round, tries to receive the mental image from the first student. The third student records both the drawn symbol as well as the "guess" of the subject. Have the students try this experience in several ways:

1) shuffling the deck, then going through the whole deck one card at a time
2) shuffling the deck, then drawing one card at a time, replacing it and reshuffling for each trial
3) shuffling the deck, then randomly drawing one card at a time from the deck, but not replacing it or reshuffling for each trial.

Let them repeat the test each way for twenty-five draws. Then the students in each group switch roles until each group member has been a transmitter, a receiver and a recorder.

Allow groups to discuss their results.

Evaluation:

Participation, helpfulness and interest.

---

2. Left Mode

Analyze The Experience

Teacher More Active

Objective:

To enable the students to examine the process of testing their ESP abilities.

Activity:

Have each group select a reporter who will explain to the class what his/her group discovered about their ESP Reporters and class members can respond to the following discussion questions: How well did you do? Does anyone in your group have ESP? How are you able to tell? Did anyone get a perfect score (all correct)? Do you think it takes a perfect score to indicate ESP? What would be a good score (likely to have ESP)?

Teacher should then mention the concept of comparing desirable results (correct guesses) to the total number of guesses, using a ratio to compare these numbers.

Evaluation:

Quality of discussion.

QUADRANT TWO

CONCEPT FORMULATION

THE ANALYTIC LEARNER'S MOST COMFORTABLE PLACE

CONCERN FOR THE FACTS AS EXPERTS SEE THEM — TEACH IT TO THEM

Answer the question "WHAT?"

Teacher's Role — Information Giver

Method — Informational

---

3. Right Mode

Integrate Reflections Into Concepts

Teacher More Active

Objective:

To have the students experience the inaccuracy of their guesses as to the likelihood or unlikelihood of certain events.

Activity:

Ask the students to guess the probability of at least two students in the class sharing the same birthday. It would appear that this is a very unlikely event. However, in a normal sized class of twenty-five students, it is almost certain (nearly 100% probability) that there will be a pair who share a birthday. Ask each student to call off her/his birthday. If another student hears his/her birthday called, s/he should raise her/his hand. (See *Mathematics: A Human Endeavor*)[8] Of 365 days which are possible birthdates, we are considering *pairs* of birthdates. With one person, there are no pairs. With two persons, there is one pair. With three persons, there are three pairs. For each additional person in the group, another pair is added for each person already in the group. Therefore, to determine the number of pairs for a group of n members, you must add the sum of all numbers from 1 through n-1. As you can see, there are certainly more opportunities for a matching pair than appeared at first.

Now try another activity. Ask students to jot down a number between 1 and 50. If you have a group of up to 15 students there will be a 90% probability that two students will select a pair of matching numbers. (For smaller classes refer to the chart in *Mathematics: A Human Endeavor* Teachers' Edition to determine the correct range.)[9] Students will usually assume that it is fairly unlikely for a pair of students to select the same number. Have students call out their numbers as with the birthdays to see if any pairs exist. For larger classes, extend the range.

Now ask the students what these two examples demonstrate about probability. There is likely to be a variety of responses. If no one makes the point that we must have some standard procedures to determine the probability of certain events, the teacher should stress this, and tell the students that the purpose of this unit is to learn about these concepts and procedures. Probability is a ratio comparing the frequency of events to the total number of events. The underlying problem in most cases is to determine these numbers.

Evaluation:

Quality of discussion and accuracy of understanding.

4. Left Mode

Develop Theories And Concepts

Teacher More Active

Objective:

To make students aware of the basic concepts of probability.

Activity:

Teacher lectures on the following topics: definition of probability, sample space, equally likely events, complementary events, odds, independent events, dependent events, event, theoretical probability, experimental probability, textbook readings and assignments.

Evaluation:

Objective test.

QUADRANT THREE

PRACTICE AND PERSONALIZATION

THE COMMON SENSE LEARNER'S MOST COMFORTABLE PLACE

CONCERN FOR HANDS-ON EXPERIENCE — LET THEM TRY IT

Answer the question "HOW DOES THIS WORK?"

Teacher's Role — Coach/Facilitator

Method — Facilitation

---

5. Left Mode

Working On Defined Concepts

(Reinforcement and Manipulation)

Students More Active

Objective:

To give the students additional practice in solving probability problems.

Activity:

Workbooks, worksheets and textbook problems.

Evaluation:

Quality and accuracy of the above.

---

6. Right Mode

"Messing Around"

(Adding Something of Themselves)

Students More Active

Objective:

To allow the students to try several hands-on experiments and compare the calculated experimental probability to the theoretical probability.

Activity:

The teacher sets up a series of experiment stations. Students are instructed to write a report on each experiment. The report must include a short description of what event is being examined in which the students should describe the favorable event in the experiment,

figure out the theoretical probability of that favorable event,

perform the experiment 20 times and record results,

calculate the experimental probability based on results,

write a short analysis of the results.

Compare the theoretical and experimental probabilities. If there is a great discrepancy, how can it be accounted for? What other factors influenced the results?

The experiments for each station are as follows:
Rolling a single die to come up with "5".
Drawing a certain colored marble from a jar containing a mixture of several marbles in various colors.
Flipping a coin to come up "heads."
Drawing a face card from a deck of 52 playing cards.

Evaluation:

Quality of the reports.

QUADRANT FOUR

INTEGRATING APPLICATION AND EXPERIENCE

THE DYNAMIC LEARNER'S MOST COMFORTABLE PLACE

CONCERN FOR ACTION, DOING — LET THEM TEACH IT TO THEMSELVES AND SHARE WHAT THEY LEARN WITH OTHERS

Answer the questions
"WHAT CAN THIS BECOME?"
"WHAT CAN I MAKE OF THIS?"

Teacher's Role — Evaluator/Remediator

Method — Self-Discovery

---

7. Left Mode

Analyzing Their Own Application Of The Concepts For Usefulness, Originality, And As A Stepping Stone For Future Learning

Students More Active

Objective:

To have students select a particular application of probability theory, and to investigate this application.

Activity:

Give the students the following four options of which they must choose one and write a report:

Research the uses of probability in gambling. How do casinos know that they are going to make money? How do casinos set the odds? Go to the library for information on this subject, or write to a Nevada casino for information. Talk to a local church or civic group that runs Bingo or other charitable gambling events.

Survey your classmates about some of their genetic traits. Sample the students in this class about various traits which they inherited genetically. Some possible traits to consider include: left/right handedness, connected or nonconnected ear lobes, ability to roll the tongue, color blindness, blood types, hair or eye color. Using your results project the probability that such traits will occur in the general population. See if you can determine some actual statistics from the research section of the library. If your results are different from the listed statistics, state why you think this occurred.

Study the use of probability in the insurance business. Get a copy of *I Hate Mathematics!* by Marilyn Burns and Martha Hairston[10]. Read the section entitled "The Birthday Insurance Company" on page 111. Write a report considering the questions posed in the article. Expand the report by talking to an insurance agent, an actuary, or someone who is involved in setting up insurance policies, so you can get first hand information on how probability and statistics are involved in these fields.

Open your eyes and ears and locate some other application for probability theory in business or science. You must have your topic approved by the teacher.

Evaluation:

The level of the students' involvement.

8. Right Mode

Doing It Themselves And Sharing What They Do With Others

(Integrating Application and Experience)

Students More Active

Objective:

To allow the students to share what has been learned regarding their applications of probability.

Activity:

Students complete their investigations as described above. Each student must prepare a presentation of his/her findings. Acceptable presentations include: a research report, an oral report to the class, a model, display or simulation, a short film or photo essay, other creative approaches as approved by teacher.

Evaluation:

Quality of the above.

The Complete 4MAT System Model

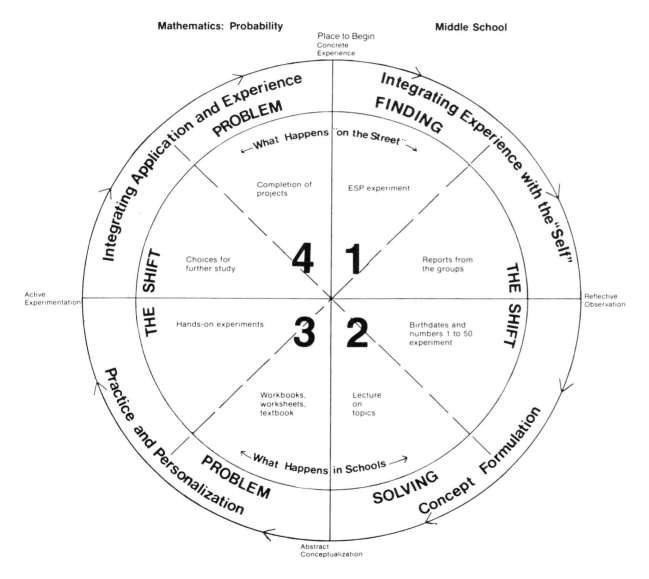

Mathematics: Probability

Middle School

Place to Begin
Concrete
Experience

Integrating Application and Experience

PROBLEM

Integrating Experience with the "Self"

FINDING

←What Happens on the Street→

Completion of projects

ESP experiment

THE SHIFT

4 **1**

THE SHIFT

Choices for further study

Reports from the groups

Active Experimentation

Reflective Observation

THE SHIFT

Hands-on experiments

3 **2**

Birthdates and numbers 1 to 50 experiment

Workbooks, worksheets, textbook

Lecture on topics

Practice and Personalization

PROBLEM

←What Happens in Schools→

SOLVING

Concept Formulation

Abstract
Conceptualization

AUTHOR: MARLENE WIECZOREK BOWEN

THEME: "Let us revive the American entrepreneurial spirit in seeking new energy sources and conserving the old."

Steve Bork

QUADRANT ONE

INTEGRATING EXPERIENCE WITH THE SELF

THE IMAGINATIVE LEARNER'S MOST COMFORTABLE PLACE

CONCERN WITH PERSONAL MEANING — CREATE A REASON

Answer the question "WHY?"

Teacher's Role — Motivator

Method — Simulation to encourage brainstorming for imagination, innovation, and empathy

---

1. Right Mode

Create An Experience

Teacher More Active

Objective:

To enhance student curiosity about the energy consumption levels of his/her family.

To increase group processing skills.

Activity:

Assign the students to groups of four. Hand out the following worksheets:

1. The "Energy Saver's Checklist" (See page 186.)
2. The "Increase in Electricity in the Home" Checklist (See page 187.)
3. "The Electric Bill Checklist"[11] (See page 188.)

Note:

These checklists were taken from the Allyn and Bacon *Exploring Physical Science* Series. This series contains the kind of practical, meaningful application of science so necessary for our students.

Students discuss these worksheets in their groups and take them home for completion in two days.

Evaluation:

Group work and completed checklists.

2. Left Mode

Analyze The Experience

Teacher More Active

Objective:

To examine the gathered data.

To enhance student ability to work in small groups.

To graph their combined findings.

Activity:

Discussion of energy checklists in small groups. Tasks for small groups:

1. On the "Energy Saver's Checklist" what is the average number of items checked in your group?
2. On "The Increasing Use of Electricity in the Home" checklist, what is the average number of items checked in your group for category C, category P and category G?
3. What is the average of your group for item F, "The Fuel Needed to Supply Electrical Energy" on the "Electric Bill" checklist?

Note: Separate the students who have electrically heated homes into a special group since they will unfairly increase group averages.

4. Plot the following graph for your group.

ENERGY SAVER'S CHECKLIST	USE OF ELECTRICITY			
30	102			Average fuel needed by group's families to supply electrical energy
	90			
25	80			
	70			
20	60			
				Group Names:
15	50			
	40			
10	30			
	20			
5	10			
0	0	C	P	G

5. Post the graph in the classroom.

Evaluation:

Group process and completion of graphs.

---

*Students must have prior instruction in electricity, heat, and energy.

ENERGY SAVER'S CHECKLIST

Check off the items that are practiced in your home. Is your family efficient in its use of energy? Answers will vary.

_____ 1. Set hot water heater at 43°C.

_____ 2. Set refrigerator on a not-so-cold setting.

_____ 3. Set up cartons to recycle paper, glass and metals.

_____ 4. Use lower-wattage bulbs.

_____ 5. Remove extra bulbs in ceiling fixtures.

_____ 6. Replace two 60W bulbs with one 100W; this gives more light and uses less electricity.

_____ 7. Do not use long-life bulbs; they give less light per watt.

_____ 8. Replace incandescent lights with fluorescent lights, where possible.

_____ 9. Use light-colored walls, curtains, rugs.

_____ 10. Check efficiency ratings on appliances such as refrigerators and air conditioners before purchasing.

_____ 11. Use returnable bottles.

_____ 12. Caulk and weatherstrip around doors and windows.

_____ 13. Turn off lights when leaving room.

_____ 14. Set furnace at 20°C or lower during the day, 16°C at night; set air conditioners at 25°C.

_____ 15. Clean furnace filter and get the burner serviced yearly.

_____ 16. Wash clothes in cold water.

_____ 17. Add storm windows and doors or plastic sheets over windows.

_____ 18. Insulate the house — 10 cm in walls, 15 cm in ceilings.

_____ 19. Keep garage door closed in winter if attached to house.

_____ 20. On nice days dry clothes out-of-doors instead of in a dryer.

_____ 21. Dry full loads in dryer.

_____ 22. Check gasoline economy of car; tune regularly.

_____ 23. Drive under 90 kilometers per hour.

_____ 24. Buy products made of recycled materials such as recycled paper.

_____ 25. Walk or ride a bike for short trips.

_____ 26. Buy products of natural materials instead of manufactured materials such as plastic (which require more energy to produce).

_____ 27. Shop at businesses which make an effort to conserve energy and resources.

_____ 28. Encourage parents and others to use a car pool whenever possible.

_____ 29. Turn down the thermostat if everyone is leaving the house for several hours.

_____ 30. Shut off the furnace pilot light during the summer.

The "Energy Saver's Checklist"
Allyn and Bacon © **1981**

THE INCREASING USE OF ELECTRICITY IN THE HOME

Compare the number of electrical devices used in three successive generations. Use this list to record the appliances in your home. Indicate these with a C (child). Then have a parent indicate those that were in the home when they were your age with a P (parent). Finally indicate those your grandparents had with a G (grandparent).

Electrical Appliance	Number of Each
1. Air conditioner, central	_____
2. Air conditioner, room units	_____
3. Battery charger	_____
4. Baby bottle warmer	_____
5. Beanpot	_____
6. Blanket	_____
7. Blender	_____
8. Broiler (portable)	_____
9. Electric broom	_____
10. Can opener	_____
11. Coffeemaker	_____
12. Comb	_____
13. Clock	_____
14. Defroster for refrigerator	_____
15. Dehumidifier	_____
16. Dishwasher	_____
17. Disposer, food waste	_____
18. Door bell	_____
19. Drill	_____
20. Dryer, clothes (or gas)	_____
21. Fan	_____
22. Fingernail buffer	_____
23. Floor waxer	_____
24. Food warmer tray	_____
25. Freezer (independent unit)	_____
26. Fryer, deep fat	_____
27. Frypan	_____
28. Garage door	_____
29. Griddle	_____
30. Grill, outdoor	_____
31. Guitar	_____
32. Hairbrush	_____
33. Haircurlers	_____
34. Hair curling iron	_____
35. Hair dryer, standing or portable	_____
36. Heater, room	_____
37. Heating pad	_____
38. Hedge trimmers	_____
39. Hot dog cooker	_____
40. Humidifier	_____
41. Ice cream maker	_____
42. Ice crusher	_____
43. Intercom system	_____
44. Iron, regular or steam	_____
45. Kiln, ceramic	_____
46. Knife	_____
47. Knife sharpener	_____
48. Lamp(s), standard	_____
49. Lamp, heat	_____
50. Lamp, sun	_____
51. Lathe	_____
52. Lawn edger & trimmer	_____
53. Lawnmower	_____
54. Lights, indoor night	_____
55. Lights, indoor wall fixture	_____
56. Lights, outdoor lawn	_____
57. Manicure set	_____
58. Massager	_____
59. Mathematical calculator	_____
60. Mirror, lighted, for makeup	_____
61. Mixer	_____
62. Organ	_____
63. Oven, bun or roll warmer	_____
64. Oven, dutch	_____
65. Oven, microwave	_____
66. Oven, portable	_____
67. Oven, toaster	_____
68. Pencil sharpener	_____
69. Popcorn popper	_____
70. Projector, movie	_____
71. Projector, slide	_____
72. Radio, clock	_____
73. Radio, standard	_____
74. Range, kitchen	_____
75. Record player	_____
76. Refrigerator	_____
77. Rotisserie	_____
78. Router (tool)	_____
79. Rug shampooer	_____
80. Sander	_____
81. Saw	_____
82. Scissors	_____
83. Sewing machine	_____
84. Shaver	_____
85. Shoe polisher	_____
86. Soldering kit	_____
87. Tape recorder	_____
88. Television	_____
89. Thermostat (oil or gas heat)	_____
90. Toaster	_____
91. Toothbrush	_____
92. Train set	_____
93. Typewriter	_____
94. Vacuum cleaner	_____
95. Vaporizer	_____
96. Waffle iron	_____
97. Washer, clothes	_____
98. Water heater	_____
99. Water pik	_____
100. Woodburning set	_____
101. Yogurt maker	_____
102. Other _____	_____

_____

"The Increasing Use of Electricity in the Home"
Allyn and Bacon © 1981

THE ELECTRIC BILL

Use a recent electric bill to answer the following:

A. Kilowatt-hours of electric energy used:

B. Days bill covers:

C. Energy per day for your family: $\dfrac{A}{B}$

D. Energy per day per person: $\dfrac{C}{\text{Persons in family}}$

E. Kilocalories used per person: D $\times$ 860 kilocalories

F. Fuel energy needed to supply electrical energy: $\dfrac{E}{.30}$

"The Electric Bill"
Allyn and Bacon © 1981.

QUADRANT TWO

CONCEPT FORMULATION

THE ANALYTIC LEARNER'S MOST COMFORTABLE PLACE

CONCERN FOR THE FACTS AS EXPERTS SEE THEM — TEACH IT TO THEM

Answer the question "WHAT?"

Teacher's Role — Information Giver

Method — Informational

---

3. Right Mode

Integrate Reflections Into Concepts

Teacher More Active

Objective:

To enhance understanding of the problem of energy waste.

To give opportunity to express a concept in art.

Activity:

Students are instructed to do the following: Answer these questions, then we will discuss your answers. Suppose a family has $2,000 in savings (nonrenewable). They also have $200 a week from working (renewable). How long can they spend $2,200 a week before they run out of money? $1,200 a week, $200 a week? (This exercise was taken from the Heath Series.)[12]

How long can you do hard work, for example running up steep steps, before you run out of energy? What must you do then? What if you were unable to renew your energy, what if there were little food to go around? Could you continue to run up those steps?

When you use nonrenewable energy, it is gone. Now using a large piece of art paper and magic markers, draw your concept of our world if it ran out of energy.

Evaluation:

Art work quality in terms of concept understanding.

4. Left Mode

Develop Theories And Concepts

Teacher More Active

Objective:

To enhance knowledge of subject matter. To increase note-taking and reading skills.

Activity:

Teacher lectures on: Use of energy in appliances, energy efficiency ratio, calculating the energy use of an appliance, home heating, efficiency in appliances, lighting, home insulation, American life styles. (All above topics taken from Allyn and Bacon series.)

Students read textbook chapters.

Evaluation:

Objective test.

QUADRANT THREE

PRACTICE AND PERSONALIZATION

THE COMMON SENSE LEARNER'S MOST COMFORTABLE PLACE

CONCERN FOR HANDS-ON EXPERIENCE — LET THEM TRY IT

Answer the question "HOW DOES THIS WORK?"

Teacher's Role — Coach/Facilitator

Method — Facilitation

5. Left Mode

Working On Defined Concepts

(Reinforcement and Manipulation)

Students More Active

Objective:

To reinforce materials by practice.

Activity:

Worksheets on lecture materials, workbooks, and chapter questions.

Evaluation:

Quality of the above.

6. Right Mode

"Messing Around"

(Adding Something of Themselves)

Students More Active

Objective:

To personalize the material being learned.

Activity:

Students submit a plan to increase the energy efficiency of their homes. It should list what they can reasonably do to improve energy efficiency and reduce waste. Parents must sign this proposal.

Evaluation:

Quality of proposal, how reasonable, how possible.

QUADRANT FOUR

INTEGRATING APPLICATION AND EXPERIENCE

THE DYNAMIC LEARNER'S MOST COMFORTABLE PLACE

CONCERN FOR ACTION, DOING — LET THEM TEACH IT TO THEMSELVES AND SHARE WHAT THEY LEARN WITH OTHERS

Answer the questions
"WHAT CAN THIS BECOME?"
"WHAT CAN I MAKE OF THIS?"

Teacher's Role — Evaluator/Remediator

Method — Self-Discovery

7. Left Mode

Analyzing Their Own Application Of The Concepts For Usefulness, Originality, And As A Stepping Stone For Future Learning

Students More Active

Objective:

To enhance student ability to deal with unforeseen obstacles.

To extrapolate problems to larger society.

Activity:

Discussion (one class period) on difficulties encountered in attempting to improve energy efficiency in their homes. Extrapolate to larger society. After the discussion, students write essays on the problems they are encountering in their attempts to improve the energy efficiency in their homes.

Evaluation:

Quality of discussion and essays.

8. Right Mode

Doing It Themselves And Sharing What They Do With Others

(Integrating Application and Experience)

Students More Active

Objective:

To follow through on a plan and examine results in terms of goals.

To share their experiences with each other.

Activity:

Students carry out their plans and return to their original group of four to report on success/lack of success. Group plots a post graph. Use the same graph plotted in step two. Only graph the "Energy Saver's" checklist (the 30 items). Check for improvements in pre and post graph. Post the second graph alongside the first. Each group reports to the entire class.

Evaluation:

Posted graphs, group work and group reports.

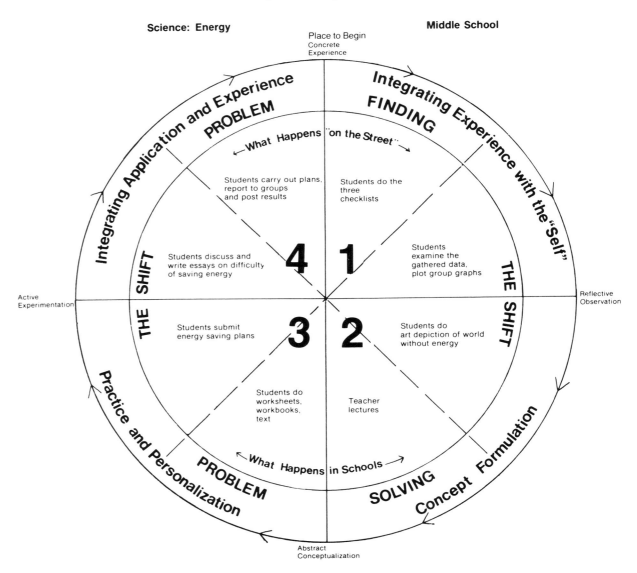

The Complete 4MAT System Model

Science: Energy

Middle School

High School Units

Social Studies/Literature: .... Bernice McCarthy
Rise Of Modern America

Law: Due Process .... Cindy Kelly

Mathematics: Algebra II: Concept Of Function ... Marilyn and Peter Tantillo

Biology: Respiration/Breathing: .... Marlene Wieczorek Bowen
The Exchange Of Gases

Unit:
Social Studies/Literature

Subject:
Rise of Modern America

Grade Level:
High School

AUTHOR: BERNICE McCARTHY

THEME: "Are we the eagle nation Milton saw
moving its mighty youth,
soon to possess the mountain words
of truth, and be a swift familiar of
the sun?"   Moody

QUADRANT ONE

INTEGRATING EXPERIENCE WITH THE SELF

THE IMAGINATIVE LEARNER'S MOST
COMFORTABLE PLACE

CONCERN WITH PERSONAL MEANING —
CREATE A REASON

Answer the question "WHY?"

Teacher's Role — Motivator

Method — Simulation to encourage brainstorming for imagination, innovation, and empathy

---

1. Right Mode

Create An Experience

Teacher More Active

Objective:

To foster appreciation of positive/negative forces
that our ancestors faced during the rise of
modern America.

To foster group planning skills.

To foster group interaction skills.

Activity:

To plan a trip working in small groups.

You and two other people are traveling on
horseback. You leave from your present home,
destination West. Time of trip: one year. You
have all the supplies you need. Money between
the three of you, $100. It is 1850.
Suggestions: maps, list of supplies, medicine,
food, clothing, cooking utensils (and remember
your horses' needs). Someone brings a musical
instrument. What might it be? What songs would
you be singing? What topics of conversation
might there be around your campfires? Someone should keep a journal. What difficulties on
the trip can you imagine? How would you
communicate with the people back home?

Check area libraries for newspapers on micro-
film 1840-1850.

Evaluation:

Participation — service to the group. Finished
product: routes, lists of supplies, and answers
to above questions. Grade for quality of group
presentation.

2. Left Mode

Analyze The Experience

Teacher More Active

Objective:

To have students reflect together on the experience.

To develop listening skills, group discussion

techniques, opinion giving and empathy for our
ancestors.

To understand the teacher's beliefs in the
importance of studying American literature and
history as well as the connections between the
two as a force in increasing self-awareness.

Activity:

Discussion of "trips."

Rules:

Only one person can speak at a time.
All opinions are acceptable if speaker gives
reasons.
Thinking out loud is acceptable.
Personal statements must be written on the
experience.

Evaluation:

Students make lists of insights gained from the
experience and rank them in priority order and
explain why. Grade for quality of personal
statements.

QUADRANT TWO

CONCEPT FORMULATION

THE ANALYTIC LEARNER'S MOST COMFORTABLE PLACE

CONCERN FOR THE FACTS AS EXPERTS SEE THEM — TEACH IT TO THEM

Answer the question "WHAT?"

Teacher's Role — Information Giver

Method — Informational

---

3. Right Mode

Integrate Reflections Into Concepts

Teacher More Active

Objective:

To read a period piece of literature.

To integrate personal reflections with the piece.

Activity:

Students read "Pioneers, O Pioneers" by Walt Whitman before class. Teacher gives lecture on Whitman. Students write essays on the poem.

Evaluation:

Essay on Whitman's poem; grade for analysis skills and writing ability. Students are required

to integrate their reflections on the "trip" experience with their essay.

4. Left Mode

Develop Theories And Concepts

Teacher More Active

Objective:

To listen to lectures and increase note-taking skills.

To ask relevant questions.

To examine facts and information.

To read critically.

To write analytically.

Activity:

Teacher gives a series of lectures:

Intellectual currents of period:
  the freedom/lawlessness of the frontier;
  war mania;
  belief in future greatness: adolescent America
    flexing its muscles.
Social and economic problems:
  race relations;
  expansion of industry and agriculture;
  growth of cities;
  labor organizations.
Readings assigned to students during this phase:
"The Psalm of the West" Lanier
"Song of the Open Road" Whitman
"The Big Rock Candy Mountain" (song)
"Casey Jones" (song)
"The Significance of the Frontier in American
  History" Frederick Jackson Turner
"Self-Reliance" Emerson
My Antonia Willa Cather.

Evaluation:

Objective test on lecture with essay questions on readings.

QUADRANT THREE

PRACTICE AND PERSONALIZATION

THE COMMON SENSE LEARNER'S MOST COMFORTABLE PLACE

CONCERN FOR HANDS-ON EXPERIENCE — LET THEM TRY IT

Answer the question "HOW DOES THIS WORK?"

Teacher's Role — Coach/Facilitator

Method — Facilitation

---

5. Left Mode

Working On Defined Concepts

(Reinforcement and Manipulation)

Students More Active

Objective:

To reinforce information through manipulation of materials.

Activity:

Workbooks, text with chapter-end questions, studying class notes. TV-watching assignments: *Little House on the Prairie, The Chisholms.*

Movies: *Westward Ho the Wagons* or check local theater and TV listings for the three-week period. Mini-lectures accompanied by overhead transparencies.

Evaluation:

Multiple choice tests, speeches to class by students on movies seen, TV, etc.

6. Right Mode

"Messing Around"

(Adding Something of Themselves)

Students More Active

Objective:

To personalize unit material.

To enhance student creativity.

To enhance students' ability to find resource information and materials.

To enhance students' understanding of community resources.

Activity:

Planning individual personalization of material. The students are required to choose a personal learning activity that will enhance and reflect their knowledge of the material under study. This is where learning styles can easily be observed.

The Innovative Learners might choose:
a play, debate, group project, art work of all kinds, letters from relative abroad, old photographs depicting the problems and freedoms of the period.

The Analytic Learners might choose:
an extended essay on some topic, researched and including lecture notes, another book to read and critique.

The Common Sense Learners might choose:
table contour maps of wagon train routes, Indian tribes who were affected by "being in the way", railroad routes, or extra work sheets from textbook.

The Dynamic Learners might choose:
creative projects of all kinds, imaginary journals, songs, poetry.

This step is a planning step. The students are asked to decide how they are going to personalize what they have learned. The plans are to detail steps, resources needed, finished product, and why they have chosen that particular plan.

Evaluation:

Individual personalization plans.

QUADRANT FOUR

INTEGRATING APPLICATION AND EXPERIENCE

THE DYNAMIC LEARNER'S MOST COMFORTABLE PLACE

CONCERN FOR ACTION, DOING — LET THEM TEACH IT TO THEMSELVES AND SHARE WHAT THEY LEARN WITH OTHERS

Answer the questions
"WHAT CAN THIS BECOME?"
"WHAT CAN I MAKE OF THIS?"

Teacher's Role — Evaluator/Remediator

Method — Self-Discovery

---

7. Left Mode

Analyzing Their Own Application Of The Concepts For Usefulness, Originality, And As A Stepping Stone For Future Learning

Students More Active

Objective:

Enhance student ability to analyze their own plans for:
1. limits (is the scope too big or too small?)
2. details (have they been specific enough?)
3. originality (is this their own?)
4. relevance (does it tell something about the unit under study?)
5. usefulness (what will they learn?)

Activity:

Students post their plan analysis
or
tell the class their plan analysis
or
write the analysis for the teacher's approval.

It is extremely helpful for all the class to hear the teacher's suggestions for improving personalization activities.

Evaluation:

Analysis of plan, work habits, research methods.

8. Right Mode

Doing It And Applying What They Have Learned To New, More Complex Experiences

Students More Active

Objective:

To complete their personal learning project. To display or explain their projects.

To share what they have learned with the other students.

Activity:

Students work on their projects, display them, or explain them, and share what they have learned with the other students.

Evaluation:

Projects graded for originality, ability to typify period under study, use of resources, and method of presentation to other students.

To end the unit, the teacher inaugurates a discussion of "Where do we go from here?" This discussion would include: areas for future study, evaluative student feedback, ideas about the next Concrete Experience, etc. The discussion, the class reactions, the material still to be covered and the teacher's plans form the nucleus for the next unit.

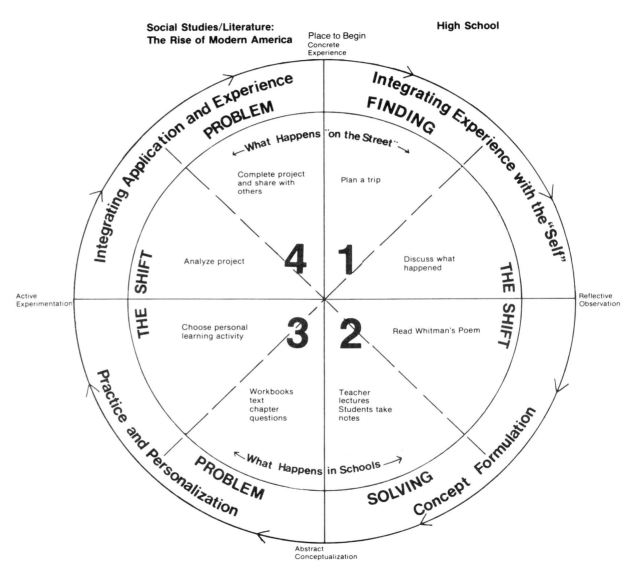

The Complete 4MAT System Model

Social Studies/Literature: The Rise of Modern America — High School

Subject: Law Unit: Due Process Grade Level: High School

AUTHOR: CINDY KELLY

THEME: "The dividing line between government's functions and the individual's rights, privileges and inescapable responsibilities is never completely fixed; never is static. It oscillates constantly in a middle area between centralized authority and individual liberty." Dwight Eisenhower

QUADRANT ONE

INTEGRATING EXPERIENCE WITH THE SELF

THE IMAGINATIVE LEARNER'S MOST COMFORTABLE PLACE

CONCERN WITH PERSONAL MEANING — CREATE A REASON

Answer the question "WHY?"

Teacher's Role — Motivator

Method — Simulation to encourage brainstorming for imagination, innovation, and empathy

---

1. Right Mode

Create An Experience

Teacher More Active

Objective:

To enhance student understanding that due process is a concept that applies to students.

Activity:

Teacher announces the following new classroom rules:

1. Any student who misses more than one class a semester will receive a "D."
2. Any student who interrupts another student will be suspended from class for three days.
3. The teacher has the final authority to decide what rules will apply in the classroom. Students who are unhappy can drop the class; however, they will receive an "F."

Teacher asks the students to write their reactions to these rules, or they can discuss their reactions in small groups, then give a report to the class on group consensus.

Evaluation:

Quality of reactions.

2. Left Mode

Analyze The Experience

Teacher More Active

Objective:

To have students recognize the importance of understanding the concept of due process.

Activity:

Teacher leads the discussion focusing on the following questions: Are these rules fair? Why or why not? What other school rules are unfair? How can students challenge rules they consider to be unfair? What procedures should exist to protect students who feel they are treated unfairly by teachers?
Personal Witness: the teacher should sum up the discussion with a carefully thought out statement on her/his own feelings/experiences concerning due process. This step is of vital importance. If a teacher does not personally value the material to be taught and therefore cannot witness that value, s/he should not be teaching the course.

Evaluation:

Quality of discussion.

QUADRANT TWO

CONCEPT FORMULATION

THE ANALYTIC LEARNER'S MOST COMFORTABLE PLACE

CONCERN FOR THE FACTS AS EXPERTS SEE THEM — TEACH IT TO THEM

Answer the question "WHAT?"

Teacher's Role — Information Giver

Method — Informational

---

3. Right Mode

Integrate Reflections Into Concepts

Teacher More Active

Objective:

To integrate the previous experience and reflections (discussion) into the concept of due process.

197

Activity:

Students read the following fact situation and respond to the questions posed (hypothetical student suspension).

Mr. Monroe, the seventh-grade teacher assigned to cafeteria duty, came upon a food fight in process. Before he could get across the crowded room to intervene, the food fight turned into a fist fight involving several students. Although the fight broke up as he approached the area, he ordered all the students at the table to report to the principal. The principal explained that all the students were to be suspended for three days because of their disruptive conduct. Jerry replied that he had merely been sitting at the table and he had not taken part. He demanded a hearing in order to question Mr. Monroe, and to have his friends testify in his behalf. After listening to Jerry, the principal decided that he was lying. He told Jerry that he believed Mr. Monroe and that Jerry had just had his hearing. Jerry responded that he knew he was entitled to due process rights before suspension, and that he could sue the principal for violating his constitutional rights. Is he correct?

Teacher asks students to identify the arguments which the principal would use to support his actions and the arguments that Jerry would make. What facts support each position? What constitutional provisions apply?

Evaluation:

Quality of response and understanding of conflicts involved.

4. Left Mode

Develop Theories And Concepts

Teacher More Active

Objective:

To understand the constitutional requirements for the application of due process and to understand that due process is a flexible concept.

Activity:

Students read the Fifth and Fourteenth Amendments to the Constitution. Teacher delivers lecture outlining the requirements for due process to apply:

There must be state action and deprivation of life, liberty, and/or property interest. Teacher should ask students for their definition of due process, and then outline the most expansive definition (provided in a criminal trial).

QUADRANT THREE

PRACTICE AND PERSONALIZATION

THE COMMON SENSE LEARNER'S MOST COMFORTABLE PLACE

CONCERN FOR HANDS-ON EXPERIENCE — LET THEM TRY IT

Answer the question "HOW DOES THIS WORK?"

Teacher's Role — Coach/Facilitator

Method — Facilitation

5. Left Mode

Working On Defined Concepts

(Reinforcement and Manipulation)

Students More Active

Objective:

Reinforcement of information.

Activity:

Students role play situations on pages 201 to 206 and other students serve as judges determining whether the individual's due process rights were recognized in each case.

Evaluation:

Quality of participation and opinion reasoning.

6. Right Mode

"Messing Around"

(Adding Something of Themselves)

Students More Active

Objective:

To integrate material with a personal expression of learning.

Activity:

Students develop hypothetical situations for other students to analyze to determine whether a student's due process rights were recognized. (Example: A teacher reduces a student's grade because s/he had an unexcused absence as a result of a day at the zoo to entertain grandparents who arrived unexpectedly.)

Evaluation:

Quality of hypotheticals.

QUADRANT FOUR

INTEGRATING APPLICATION AND EXPERIENCE

THE DYNAMIC LEARNER'S MOST COMFORTABLE PLACE

CONCERN FOR ACTION, DOING — LET THEM TEACH IT TO THEMSELVES AND SHARE WHAT THEY LEARN WITH OTHERS

Answer the questions
"WHAT CAN THIS BECOME?"
"WHAT CAN I MAKE OF THIS?"

Teacher's Role — Evaluator/Remediator

Method — Self-Discovery

7. Left Mode

Analyzing Their Own Application Of The Concepts For Usefulness, Originality, And As A Stepping Stone For Future Learning

Students More Active

Objective:

To develop a method for applying due process in student's own environment.

Activity:

Students *examine* school discipline codes and other rules/regulations to determine whether they are consistent with due process requirements.

Evaluation:

Quality of analysis.

8. Right Mode

Doing It Themselves And Sharing What They Do With Others

(Integrating Application and Experience)

Students More Active

Objective:

To teach other students what they have learned; to *apply* due process concept in student's own environment.

Activity:

Students work in groups or as individuals to develop a model set of classroom and school rules that are consistent with due process concepts. Students present their models in class and class votes to adopt the model they feel is most applicable. Students draft a model discipline code and present it to student council, principal, or other appropriate body/person for review and implementation.

Evaluation:

Quality of finished product and participation.

The Complete 4MAT System Model

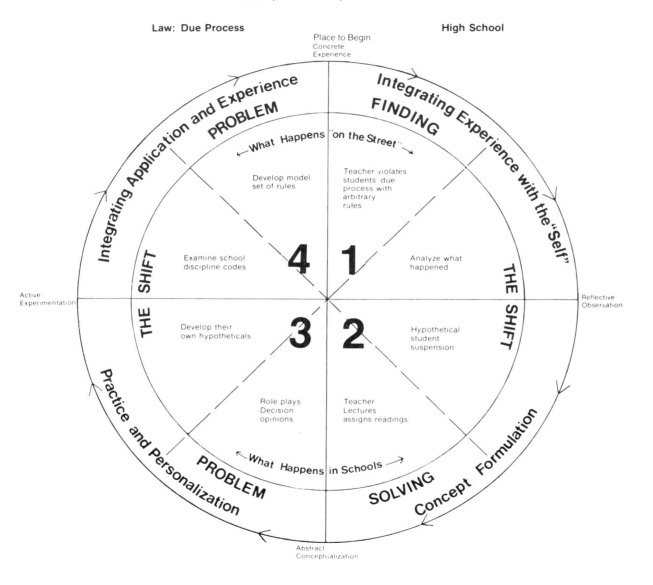

Law: Due Process   High School

Place to Begin
Concrete
Experience

Integrating Application and Experience
PROBLEM

Integrating Experience with the "Self"
FINDING

← What Happens "on the Street" →

Develop model set of rules

Teacher violates students' due process with arbitrary rules

THE SHIFT

4

1

THE SHIFT

Examine school discipline codes

Analyze what happened

Active Experimentation

Reflective Observation

3

2

Develop their own hypotheticals

Hypothetical student suspension

Practice and Personalization

Role plays Decision opinions

Teacher Lectures assigns readings

Concept Formulation

PROBLEM

← What Happens in Schools →

SOLVING

Abstract Conceptualization

Role Plays for Due Process Lesson

SKIT ONE

The Players: Sandy Kelly
Mrs. Kelly, Sandy's Mother;
Candy, Sandy's friend;
Mandy, Candy's friend;
Mr. Allright, principal of high school;
Mrs. Smith, mother of Marilou Smith;
Marilou Smith, another student.

SCENE ONE: Mrs. Kelly's kitchen. Mrs. Kelly is sitting at the table, elbows propped up having a cup of coffee. The time is 3:15. The door bursts open. Sandy Kelly comes rushing in with her two friends, Candy and Mandy.

Mrs. Kelly: (shocked when she looks at the state the girls are in)

Girls! What on earth has happened? What's wrong...tell me, what's the matter?

Sandy: (controlling her breath with great difficulty) Oh...Momma ... we just saw the awfullest thing! (Moans) Oh! just the awfullest thing!

Mrs. Kelly: (using a controlled, quiet voice)

Now calm down girls, just sit right down here by me, and tell me what has happened.

Candy: (equally as breathless as Sandy)
We just saw that bunch of girls from over on eighth street . . .

you know, that tough bunch of girls . . . oh (moans)

Mrs. Kelly: Yes, saw what?

Candy: (continuing after swallowing hard)
We just saw that bunch of girls . . . beat up the two new students . . . you know . . . the two new girls who just moved in last week. Oh gosh, it was terrible!

Mrs. Kelly: What do you mean, beat up? (she must repeat the question, as the girls are too upset to answer) Girls, what do you mean, beat up?

Mandy: (speaking very quickly)
Well . . . they knocked them down . . . right on the sidewalk . . . and . . . hit them with their books . . . broke one of the girl's glasses . . . (gulps) and took all their stuff!

Mrs. Kelly: (hands up to her face)
Good Lord! Couldn't you help them? Couldn't you help those poor girls?

Sandy: No Momma . . . we couldn't . . . there were too many of them . . . (pauses, lowers her voice) and, . . . I guess we were too afraid.

Mrs. Kelly: (very quiet and thoughtful now)
Have some coke and cookies girls. We'll talk about this later. Now just calm down, you did

what you could, just calm down.

SCENE TWO

Mrs. Kelly is on the telephone. She is alone in the room. She is talking to Mr. Allright, the school principal.

Mrs. Kelly: Yes, of course, the girls will tell what they saw; we feel those girls should be punished severely for what they did.

(pauses and listens)
No thanks necessary, Mr. Allright. We understand the board needs witnesses.

(pauses again)
No, we're not afraid. I've talked to the other parents and we want our girls to do what's right.

SCENE THREE

Mr. Allright's office.

Mr. Allright: I see, Mrs. Kelly. Your daughter, Mandy, and Candy have heard the alleged assailants talking about reprisals on anyone who testifies against them. But let me calm your fears. No one knows who our witnesses are. I do understand your nervousness, but I certainly hope the girls will testify.

Mrs. Kelly:	They have prepared statements and will submit them to the board for the expulsion hearing. But (with emphasis) they will remain unsigned. My daughter and her friends must remain anonymous. The girls are terrified, and I don't blame them. The other parents and my husband and I have agreed to do it this way.
Mr. Allright:	(looking disappointed) I understand, Mrs. Kelly, that will just have to do.
SCENE FOUR	Mr. Allright's office. Mrs. Smith and her daughter Marilou are seated in front of the principal's desk.
Mr. Allright	(speaking firmly) I'm sorry, Mrs. Smith, but the decision stands. The nature of the offense is so severe. Marilou is expelled. That is the irrevocable decision of the board.
Marilou:	(very upset voice, almost in tears) Mr. Allright, I wasn't there. I wasn't with those girls when they did what they did. I swear, I wasn't with those girls!
Mr. Allright:	We have signed statements from eyewitnesses that indeed, Marilou, you were there. You were with them.
Mrs. Smith:	I do not think this is fair, Mr. Allright, not at all fair. We were never allowed to question those witnesses. Weren't we supposed to get the chance to question them, when they claim they saw my Marilou do such a terrible thing?
Mrs. Kelly:	Mrs. Smith, there was some question of the safety of our witnesses and you can understand why they insisted on remaining anonymous! (pauses and lowers his voice.) I'm sorry, the expulsion stands.
Mrs. Smith:	(standing up) Come, Marilou. Good day, Mr. Allright, you'll be hearing from our attorney.

SKIT TWO

The Players: Sam White, a student;
Mr. McDonald, an employee of the school district;
Mr. White, Sam's father;
Mrs. White, Sam's mother.

SCENE ONE

Sam is sitting in his car listening to the radio. The car is parked on a street adjacent to the high school campus. The time is just before first class in the morning. Mr. McDonald, who is walking by, sees Sam and walks up to the car window.

Mr. McDonald: Hi Sam, how are you this morning?

Sam: Good, just listening to the end of this song. I love this group, this is their best song.

Mr. McDonald: (glances at the tape deck, sees a small bag resting there, nods towards the bag.) That bag belong to you Sam?

Sam: (looks nervous) Yes sir, it does.

Mr. McDonald: (pauses a moment, looks more severe) That marijuana, Sam?

Sam: (waits a moment, then says) Yes sir, it is.

Mr. McDonald: Sam, I'm going to have to report this.

Sam: (looking amazed) I'm not bringing it into school. It's just sitting here in my car.

Mr. McDonald: 'Fraid that's still against the rules, Sam.

SCENE TWO: Sam's kitchen. Mr. and Mrs. White, Sam's parents, are sitting at the kitchen. There is a letter on the table. Sam walks in.

Mr. White: Hi, Sam, sit down. We've got a letter here from school. It says you've been expelled for the entire quarter.

Sam: (looking very ashamed) I know, Dad, I came home to tell you.

Mrs. White: Sam, how could you? How much marijuana did you have in your car and why on earth did you bring it to school?

Sam: Mom, I had a fourteenth of an ounce and I didn't bring it to school. It was in my car. I had no intention of bringing it to school.

Mr. White: (amazed tone of voice) In your car? Where was your car parked?

Sam: On Atkins Street.

Mr. White: On Atkins Street? Not on school property?

Sam: Right, Dad. But the principal told me the school campus takes in maybe eight or nine blocks. He says anyone within 500 feet of the campus is considered on school property.

Mr. White: I wonder if all those folks on Atkins Street know they're living on school property.

Mrs. White: (looks at her husband disapprovingly for making a joke at such an inopportune time) Sam, does the student handbook say that the campus includes all property within 500 feet of the school?

Sam: No, Mom, it sure doesn't.

Mr. White: Sam, I sure wish you wouldn't fool around with marijuana at all. But, I'll be darned if they can make this stick. I sure don't see how the school board can expel you for having marijuana in your car on Atkins Street. Get me the phone book. We're not going to take this. We're going to see a lawyer.

SKIT THREE

The Players: Johnny Kumlately, student;
                Rebecca, a student;
                Mr. Kamereye, a photography
                  teacher;
                Mrs. Letterite, a business
                  English teacher;
                Coach McGraw, a phsyical
                  education teacher;
                Dean Ruhlbook, Dean of
                  Discipline;
                Mr. Kumlately, Johnny's father.

SCENE ONE: Hall of a large high school.
                Students busily coming and
                going, opening and closing
                lockers. Johnny Kumlately
                walks to his locker. He is
                scowling. Rebecca, a friend of
                his, is closing her locker right
                next to Johnny's.

Rebecca: Hi Johnny. Where've you
                been? Boy, you look mad.

Johnny: Just been to Ruhlbook's office.
                He refused to give me an
                excused absence for the two
                days I was gone. Boy! what a
                deal. What a stupid rule!

Rebecca: Boy you know it. That means
                they'll lower your grades?

                (Johnny nods)
                Oh, Johnny did ya think
                they'd do it?

Johnny: I didn't even think about the
                stupid rule. I'm gonna talk to
                all three teachers. Miss Weldon

said she wouldn't, she's OK...
but the other three?

Rebecca: Got to run Johnny, good luck,
                but I wouldn't count on it.

SCENE TWO: Dean Ruhlbook's office. The
                Dean is sitting at his desk, and
                three teachers are sitting in
                chairs around the desk: Mr.
                Kamereye, a photography
                teacher, Mrs. Letterite, a
                business English teacher, and
                Coach McGraw, a physical
                education teacher.

Dean Ruhlbook: (looking at the teachers and
                speaking in his most pro-
                fessional tone.)
                John has asked me to call this
                meeting because he is
                questioning our rule about
                unexcused absences. (lower-
                ing his voice) Notice these
                kids never question a rule
                until they break it. (looks at all
                three teachers in turn and
                says) How do you all feel
                about this?

Mr. Kamereye: (a bit hesitatingly)
                I think it's a bit harsh. John
                does well in my class.

Mrs. Letterite: (matter of factly)
                A rule's a rule.

Coach McGraw: (emphatically)
                We grade 'em on attendance.
                That's all there is to it. He
                should've been there.

Dean Ruhlbook: (smiles and speaks with firm-
                ness)

Then we agree, the rule
stands. No exceptions. John's
grades will be lowered. Do we
all agree?

Mr. Kamereye: I guess so.

Mrs. Letterite: OK.

Coach McGraw: You bet! That's what rules are
                for!

SCENE THREE: (John Kumlately's living room.
                Father and son sit talking. It is
                the end of the conversation.)

Mr. Kumlately: (speaking quietly)
                John, what can be done? It
                seems quite certain the teach-
                ers will enforce the rule.

Johnny: (firmly but with agitation in
                his voice)
                Dad, it's not fair, it's just not
                fair. I should be graded on
                what I've learned, not how
                many minutes each semester
                I sit in class. I know the
                material, I earned those grades
                fair and square. It's just not
                fair, Dad.

Mr. Kumlately: (with determination)
                I agree with you Johnny, it
                isn't fair. We'll call our lawyer,
                we'll meet them in court.

Johnny: (gleefully)
                Thanks, Dad.

SKIT FOUR

The Players: Ms. Jones, a medical student;
Professor Bones, a teacher at the medical school;
Professor Youngblood, a teacher at the medical school;
Dean Phinulwerd, the Dean of the medical school.

SCENE ONE: A classroom in a large medical school. An anatomy class is in progress.

Professor Bones: (dapper and neat, in an immaculate white coat, hand in one pocket, standing at the front of the class)
Anatomy is very important. Unfortunately there is a lot of memorization involved. So today, we're going to take the time for you to come up and give the proper terminology for our skeleton here.
(rattles skeleton as he speaks)
We'll begin with . . .

(Door opens, Ms. Jones rushes in . . . she is disheveled . . . she is breathing heavily, she rushes to her seat as the wind bangs the door shut behind her, rattling the skeleton. She reaches her seat and sits down hurridly, looking embarrassed.)

Professor Bones: (very businesslike and slowly)
My dear Ms. (emphasizing the Ms.) Jones, you are late again.

(pauses and looks at her very carefully)
And I wish to add that your appearance is less than . . . shall we say . . . professional. I will submit *another* (emphasizing) report to Dean Phinulwerd.

Ms. Jones: (stammering)
I . . . I . . . had . . . uh . . . personal reasons for being late . . . we're not children you know.

SCENE TWO: Professor Youngblood's private office. Ms. Jones has been summoned.

Professor Youngblood: Ms. Jones, this is the second time I've felt it necessary to call you in. I believe we should talk about your performance on my pediatrics ward.

Ms. Jones: Professor Youngblood, I'm very busy and I need to get back to the ward. What is it *this time*?

Professor Youngblood: I find your performance with the patients less than empathetic . . . your attendance is erratic . . . and your appearance is . . . well . . . it leaves much to be desired.

Ms. Jones: My appearance is my business, and I'm tired of hearing my looks referred to. If women are smart, it doesn't seem to be enough . . . they have to be beautiful too. I was late twice last week for duty on the ward because I was given extra

work by Professor Bones. And as for the patients, I handle them in my own personal way . . . not someone else's. (pauses) Is there anything else. I really must go.

Professor Youngblood: (snapping back)
I'll be submitting a report to Dean Phinulwerd.

Ms. Jones: (snapping back)
That's your privilege!

SCENE THREE: Dean Phinulwerd's office.

Dean: Come in Ms. Jones, sit down. The purpose of this meeting is to advise you of the decision of the Council of Evaluation. They voted this morning. Their decision was to dismiss you from the medical school.

Ms. Jones: (shocked)
Dismiss me . . . What?

Dean: (hurrying on)
As you know, the council is made up of faculty and students, your peers, and based on the number of reports submitted by various staff, the decision to dismiss you was made.

Ms. Jones: But you can't . . . you just can't. I'm almost finished.

(pauses to let the Dean's words sink in.)
Without a hearing? Don't I get a hearing? A chance to answer the charges made against me?

Dean:	(speaking slowly)
	My dear Ms. Jones, you have been informed repeatedly throughout your time here as to your unsatisfactory performance in many areas. We do not feel that another hearing is necessary. Besides, it wouldn't change anything.
Ms. Jones:	At least I would have a chance to answer the charges.
Dean:	No, I'm sorry, the decision stands.
Ms. Jones:	I refuse to accept this decision. I think it is unfair and based on prejudice against me personally.
	(stands and speaks slowly with emphasis)
	You'll be hearing from my lawyer.

Judge's Decision Sheet

Case One: (Marilou's expulsion for alleged attach on students)

Decision   For the plaintiff
(Marilou)   _____

For the defendant
(the school)   _____

Brief opinion giving reasoning:

_____

_____

_____

Case Two: (Sam and the marijuana)

Decision   For the plaintiff
(Sam)   _____

For the defendant
(the school)   _____

Brief opinion giving reasoning:

_____

_____

_____

Case Three: (Johnny and the lowered grades)

Decision   For the plaintiff
(Johnny)   _____

For the defendant
(the school)   _____

Brief opinion giving reasoning:

_____

_____

_____

Case Four: (Ms. Jones' dismissal from medical school)

Decision   For the plaintiff
(Ms. Jones)   _____

For the defendant
(the school)   _____

Brief opinion giving reasoning:

_____

_____

_____

SKIT ONE

Tibbs et al. v. Board of Education of Township of Franklin, 284 A.2d 179 (N.J. 1971)

Two female high school students were on their way home when they were attacked and robbed by a group of students from the same school. Student witnesses identified Tanya Tibbs as one of the group of attackers. When the school board held a hearing to decide whether Tanya should be expelled, however, the student witnesses were afraid of retaliation and refused to testify against Tanya. Instead, they submitted unsigned statements identifying Tanya. When Tanya was expelled on the basis of this evidence, she claimed that her due process rights were violated since she had not been able to confront her accusers. The New Jersey trial court agreed, ruling that a student who is facing expulsion must be given the opportunity to cross-examine the witnesses against him/her.

SKIT TWO

Galveston Independent School District v. Boothe, 590 S.W. 2d 553 (Texas Civ. App. 1979)

The Texas appeals court ruled that David Boothe's right to due process was violated when he was expelled. The court found that the school rules and regulations were so vague that they did not fairly notify him that expulsion could result from his possession of marijuana on a street adjacent to the campus. While it was made clear that students were not to bring marijuana "on campus," David could not have known that "on campus" meant within 500 feet of the school grounds, regardless of the offense involved.

SKIT THREE

Knight v. Board of Education Tri-Point Community Unit School District, 348 N.E.2d 299 (Ill. App. 1976)

The Illinois Appellate court ruled that the grade reduction policy did not violate the student's right to substantive due process under the Fourteenth Amendment. The court expressed its reluctance to intervene in the grading process, explaining that "where a grade is dispensed by a teacher within that teacher's subjective discretion, we can see no justification for court intervention." Although the court noted that a rule which arbitrarily reduces grades without a subjective determination of the teacher might require court intervention, this was not such a case. First, the penalty was not extremely harsh (Kevin Knight was admitted next year to a junior college, the only school to which he sought admission.) Second, the court found a rational connection between the grades and the misconduct of truancy. The court stated that most high school grading systems have comingled factors of pupil conduct with scholastic attainment in rendering grades; since truancy was conduct indicating a lack of effort, the school authorities could constitutionally consider such conduct in awarding grades.

SKIT FOUR

Board of Curators of the University of Missouri. V. Horowitz, 46 U.S.L.W. 4179 (March 1, 1978)

Charlotte Horowitz was a medical student who had an excellent academic record. However, faculty members criticized her lack of patient rapport, erratic attendance, and poor personal hygiene. In her final year, Charlotte was advised that she was being put on probation because of her clinical performance. After dissatisfactory performance the next term, the review board recommended that she be dismissed from school unless she made radical improvements. Charlotte requested that this decision be reconsidered. She was allowed to take oral and practical examinations under the supervision of seven physicians. Only two of these physicians recommended that she be allowed to graduate on schedule. After subsequent meetings of the review board, Charlotte was dismissed from medical school. She challenged this action, claiming that her due process rights were violated when she was dismissed without being given a hearing. The Supreme Court ruled that Ms. Horowitz's rights to due process had not been violated, stating that dismissals for academic reasons do not necessitate a hearing before the school's decisionmaking body.

Subject: Mathematics

Unit: Algebra II: Concept of Functions

Grade Level: High School

AUTHORS: MARILYN and PETER TANTILLO

THEME: "How can it be that mathematics, being after all a product of human thought independent of experience, is so admirably adapted to the objects of reality?" Albert Einstein

QUADRANT ONE

INTEGRATING EXPERIENCE WITH THE SELF

THE IMAGINATIVE LEARNER'S MOST COMFORTABLE PLACE

CONCERN WITH PERSONAL MEANING — CREATE A REASON

Answer the question "WHY?"

Teacher's Role — Motivator

Method — Simulation to encourage brainstorming for imagination, innovation, and empathy

---

1. Right Mode

Create An Experience

Teacher More Active

Objective:

To create student curiosity about the process of random matching function in a way that directly affects their lives.

Activity:

Draft Lottery: Have two bowls in the room, one bowl with numbers 1 to 365, another with dates January 1 to December 31. Have ten students pick a date from the first bowl and then pick a number from the second. Then in the interest of time, have the students whose birthdates have not been picked, call out their birthdates, and have a student pick from the number bowl (1 to 365) until all students' birthdates have been matched with a number from 1 to 365. (Teacher must write down birthdates of each student as s/he will need them later in the unit.)

Briefly discuss how the students feel about a random lottery deciding whether or not they are drafted. What is the purpose of a draft lottery? Why do you need to draw birthdates as well as lottery numbers? What do students know/remember about the draft lottery? In what sense is this lottery fair/unfair?

Evaluation:

Quality of discussion.

2. Left Mode

Analyze The Experience

Teacher More Active

Objective:

To allow students to analyze the lottery activity as an example of a random function.

Activity:

Discussion pertaining to the technical aspects of the lottery activity:

How many sets of elements were used? What were the elements of each set? What do the elements in each set mean? What do they stand for or represent? Is it possible that one birthdate could be assigned to two lottery numbers? What would that do to the whole process if this were so?

Have the students write brief statements about the discussion for homework.

Evaluation:

Quality of discussion and statement papers.

Note:

Steps one and two can be completed in one class period.

QUADRANT TWO

CONCEPT FORMULATION

THE ANALYTIC LEARNER'S MOST COMFORTABLE PLACE

CONCERN FOR THE FACTS AS EXPERTS SEE THEM — TEACH IT TO THEM

Answer the question "WHAT?"

Teacher's Role — Information Giver

Method — Informational

---

3. Right Mode

Integrating Reflections Into Concepts

Teacher More Active

Objective:

To create matching based on a rule.

Activity:

Teacher lists the students in rank order by birthdate. First student closest to January 1 etc. The students do not know the rankings or why. Teacher assigns the number 1 to the student whose birthday is closest to January 1 and so on. The class is asked to figure out what system the teacher used to give each of them a number. Note: If two or more students have the same birthdate, they must share the same ranking number.

After the students have figured out the why of the rankings, explain the pattern used. Ask how it is different from the ranking according to their lottery numbers. If it's possible for one birthdate to be assigned more than one ranking number? End by identifying the concepts they have experienced by their mathematical names: topics, domain, range, rule of correspondence, unique pairing or matching.

Evaluation:

Quality of discussion and understanding of the concepts.

4. Left Mode

Developing Theories And Concepts

Teacher More Active

Objective:

To teach the concepts they need to understand functions.

Activity:

Teach the following concepts: domain, range, Cartesian product and graphing, relation, rule of correspondence, function: definition of, notation, how to recognize from a graph, ordered pair, preimage (input), image (output).

Evaluation:

Objective test.

QUADRANT THREE

PRACTICE AND PERSONALIZATION

THE COMMON SENSE LEARNER'S MOST COMFORTABLE PLACE

CONCERN FOR HANDS-ON EXPERIENCE — LET THEM TRY IT

Answer the question "HOW DOES THIS WORK?"

Teacher's Role — Coach/Facilitator

Method — Facilitation

5. Left Mode

Practicing Defined "Givens"

(Reinforcement and Manipulation)

Students More Active

Objective:

To allow students to practice concepts and reinforce learning.

Activity:

Workbooks, questions at end of chapters, teacher worksheet based on lottery experience and birthdate ranking experience, graphing plotting points, etc.

Evaluation:

Quality and accuracy of worksheets.

6. Right Mode

"Messing Around"

(Adding Something of Themselves)

Students More Active

Objective:

To allow students to personalize the material.

Activity:

Students make up their own rule of correspondence. From that rule they must generate five ordered pairs. The students can either hand their worksheets to a partner or the teacher can collect them and make one large worksheet for the next class.

Evaluation:

Accuracy of ordered pairs based on student's chosen rules.

QUADRANT FOUR

INTEGRATING APPLICATION AND EXPERIENCE

THE DYNAMIC LEARNER'S MOST COMFORTABLE PLACE

CONCERN FOR ACTION, DOING — LET THEM TEACH IT TO THEMSELVES AND SHARE WHAT THEY LEARN WITH OTHERS

Answer the questions
"WHAT CAN THIS BECOME?"
"WHAT CAN I MAKE OF THIS?"

Teacher's Role — Evaluator/Remediator

Method — Self-Discovery

---

7. Left Mode

Analyzing Their Personalization For Originality And Relevance

Students More Active

Objective:

Students increase their ability to choose from options based on curiosity and interest.

Students increase their ability to write a personalized plan for learning.

To apply the concepts they have learned.

Activity:

Present the class four options. Ask them to choose one. Have them write a short essay telling why they have chosen a particular one.

The Four Options:

1. Compare statistics of accidents with the ages of people who have the most accidents. Is there a relationship? What do you conclude from this? Do you think accident statistics affect insurance rates? Is age related? Is sex related?

2. Do a survey of possible relationships between number of hours students sleep and grades, number of hours students work outside school and grades, number of hours students watch TV and grades. Note: Teacher must have this data available — a simple questionnaire *without* student names could be given to the class.

3. Scientific experiment: Obtain a lab stand and spring apparatus from your school's physical science lab. You will also need a meter stick and a set of weights of various sizes. Hang the spring with no weight attached from the lab stand, then measure the length of the unstretched spring. Attach various weights to the spring, and take a measurement of the length of the spring for each different weight. Record your data in a table in two columns, weight and length of spring.
Be sure to record the first trial — zero weight, and the unstretched length of the spring. Make a graph of the results in your table. Explain how this experiment is related to the concept of a function: (domain, range, ordered pairs, etc.)
Consult a physics teacher for alternative experiments.

4. Do a study of the following: the cost of your home, the mortgage interest rate, the number of years until it is paid. Compute the total amount your parents will have paid for your house if they live there for the length of the mortgage. Find out how the interest rate is computed. What is the rule of correspondence? Research this, use other texts, interview your parents and/or your banker.

Evaluation:

Quality of essay telling why they chose one of the above.

8. Right Mode

Doing It And Applying What They Have Learned To New, More Complex Experiences

Students More Active

Objective:

To enhance student ability to complete a project. To enable students to apply the concepts they have learned.

To share with other students.

Activity:

Complete one of the four options and share with other students.

Evaluation:

Quality of project and sharing.

The Complete 4MAT System Model

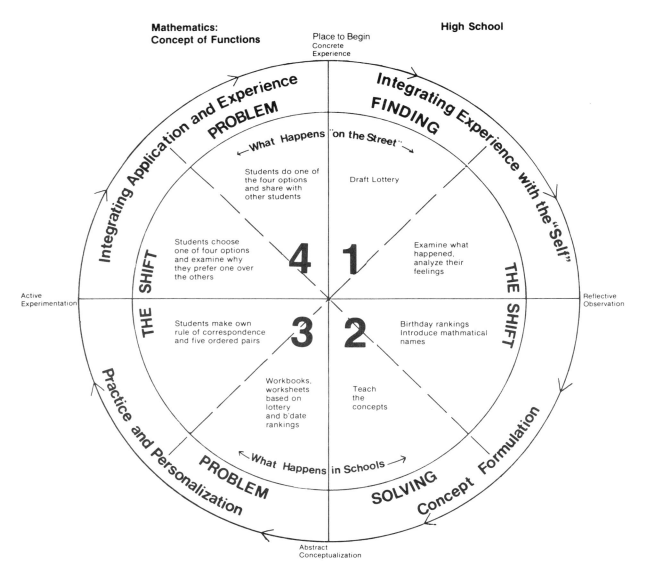

Mathematics:
Concept of Functions

High School

Place to Begin
Concrete
Experience

Integrating Application and Experience
PROBLEM

Integrating Experience with the "Self"
FINDING

← What Happens "on the Street" →

Students do one of
the four options
and share with
other students

Draft Lottery

THE SHIFT

THE SHIFT

Students choose
one of four options
and examine why
they prefer one over
the others

4 **1**

Examine what
happened,
analyze their
feelings

Active
Experimentation

Reflective
Observation

Students make own
rule of correspondence
and five ordered pairs

3 **2**

Birthday rankings
Introduce mathmatical
names

Workbooks,
worksheets
based on
lottery
and b'date
rankings

Teach
the
concepts

Practice and Personalization
PROBLEM

SOLVING
Concept Formulation

← What Happens in Schools →

Abstract
Conceptualization

Subject: Biology   Unit: Respiration/Breathing   Grade Level: High School

AUTHOR: MARLENE WIECZOREK BOWEN

THEME: "Science is organized knowledge."
Herbert Spencer

QUADRANT ONE

INTEGRATING EXPERIENCE WITH THE SELF

THE IMAGINATIVE LEARNER'S MOST COMFORTABLE PLACE

CONCERN WITH PERSONAL MEANING — CREATE A REASON

Answer the question "WHY?"

Teacher's Role — Motivator

Method — Simulation to encourage brainstorming for imagination, innovation, and empathy

---

1. Right Mode
Create An Experience

Teacher More Active

Objective:

To experience a meaningful application of the scientific knowledge of breathing and respiration.

Activity:

Have a local volunteer from the AMA or Heart Association come and give a demonstration of Cardiac Pulmonary Resuscitation, using a mannikin. Follow up the experience with a film borrowed from the same group.

Evaluation:

Attention and participation.

2. Left Mode
Analyze The Experience

Teacher More Active

Objective:

To enhance student ability to discuss what they have seen and to raise questions based on their perceptions.

To arouse their curiosity for the material to be presented.

Activity:

Discussion of what they have just experienced. Raise questions that relate to students' immediate lives — smoking, respiratory poisons, asthma, air pollutants, etc. Divide students in groups of four, hand out the following worksheet and have students answer the questions.
1. How long could you go without food?
2. How long could you go without water?
3. How long could you go without air?
4. Why do you think there is such a difference in these three?

Evaluation:

Quality of discussion and participation.

QUADRANT TWO

CONCEPT FORMULATION

THE ANALYTIC LEARNER'S MOST COMFORTABLE PLACE

CONCERN FOR THE FACTS AS EXPERTS SEE THEM — TEACH IT TO THEM

Answer the question "WHAT?"

Teacher's Role — Information Giver

Method — Informational

Right Mode
Integrating Reflections Into Concepts

Teacher More Active

Objective:

To correlate previous experience and discussion with scientific data on respiration/breathing/the exchange of gases.

Activity:

Perform experiment found in BSCS Blue Version Biology.[13] Experiment is called "Observing Change." It uses insects and plant seeds in test tubes with phenol red indicator. Live animals and plants cause a change, dead ones do not.

Give out worksheets using different examples of animals and plants. Students fill in predictions of what would happen with various indicators and why.

Evaluation:

Quality of work sheets.

4. Left Mode
Developing Theories And Concepts
Teacher More Active

Objective:

To teach concepts and theories.
To enhance note taking ability, to learn data and facts.

Activity:

Teacher lectures on: need for exchange of gases, pathway of O_2/CO_2 in mammals, mechanism for carrying O_2/CO_2 (presupposition is that material on circulatory system has been covered), structure of mammalian respiratory system, inhibitors of gas exchange (anemia, respiratory poisons, hyperventilation etc.), special cases of breathing (fetus, paralysis, asthma etc.), Text book chapter assignments. Note: Many good films available from American Lung Association, also guest speakers and literature available. American Cancer Society and Environmental Protection Agency have good lecture people for these sections on the effects of smoking and other pollutants on the quality of breathing. Community paramedics are excellent speakers.

Evaluation:

Objective Test.

QUADRANT THREE
PRACTICE AND PERSONALIZATION
THE COMMON SENSE LEARNER'S MOST COMFORTABLE PLACE

CONCERN FOR HANDS-ON EXPERIENCE — LET THEM TRY IT

Answer the question "HOW DOES THIS WORK?"

Teacher's Role — Coach/Facilitator

Method — Facilitation

---

5. Left Mode
Practicing Defined "Givens"

(Reinforcement and Manipulation)

Students More Active

Objective:

To give practice on concepts and data for further reinforcement of learning.

Activity:

Workbooks, worksheets, questions at end of chapters in textbook.

Evaluation:

Quality of the above.

6. Right Mode
"Messing Around"

(Adding Something of Themselves)

Students More Active

Objective:

To give students the opportunity to personalize the learned material by pursuing some facet that has meaning to them.

Activity:

Students begin planning a personal learning activity. (Resources must be made available.) Some suggestions:

Evaluate regulations of the Environmental Protection Agency for air quality

Evaluate quality of air on 3 preselected days in terms of breathability for (a) healthy person (b) a person with asthma, emphysema

Evaluate smoking regulations in their school, and recommend changes and revisions based on this unit

Evaluate smoking in their own lives or the lives of family members

Take a CPR course

Study the evolution of respiratory systems: earthworms, insects, fish, human respiratory systems. Make a presentation to the class with graphic charts

Research the lung system of diving mammals, make a presentation

Sketch the human respiratory system

Trace the path of an oxygen atom from the air into a body cell

Research the "bends" in divers and make class presentation with charts

Select an exercise program. Measure your height, weight, pulse (resting and exercising), blood pressure (resting and exercising) and lung capacity (resting and exercising). Keep a daily log of exercises done, time spent, and above vital signs, adding comments on efforts and effects. After six weeks evaluate exercise program in terms of its effects on you.

Evaluate various relaxation programs based on breathing exercises (yoga, TM, Lamaze, etc.). Give a summary of each, perform each for the class and present your ideas on the differences and similarities of each.

Evaluation:

Quality of student involvement.

QUADRANT FOUR

INTEGRATING APPLICATION AND EXPERIENCE

THE DYNAMIC LEARNER'S MOST COMFORTABLE PLACE

CONCERN FOR ACTION, DOING — LET THEM TEACH IT TO THEMSELVES AND SHARE WHAT THEY LEARN WITH OTHERS

Answer the questions
"WHAT CAN THIS BECOME?"
"WHAT CAN I MAKE OF THIS?"

Teacher's Role — Evaluator/Remediator

Method — Self-Discovery

7. Left Mode

Analyzing Their Personalization For Originality And Relevance

Students More Active

Objective:

To enhance their ability to systematically plan a personalized learning project.

Activity:

Students hand in their project plans including: reasons for choice, resources to be used, learning objectives, and method of sharing with the class. This could be done by individuals or groups. Teacher examines plans, revises if necessary, sets date required for completion and sets up presentation dates where necessary.

Evaluation:

Quality of plans.

8. Right Mode

Doing It And Applying What They Have Learned To New, More Complex Experiences

Students More Active

Objective:

To enhance their ability to carry out a learning plan.

To share what they learn with their classmates.

Activity:

Students complete their plans and share with their classmates.

Evaluation:

Quality of project and sharing.

The Complete 4MAT System Model

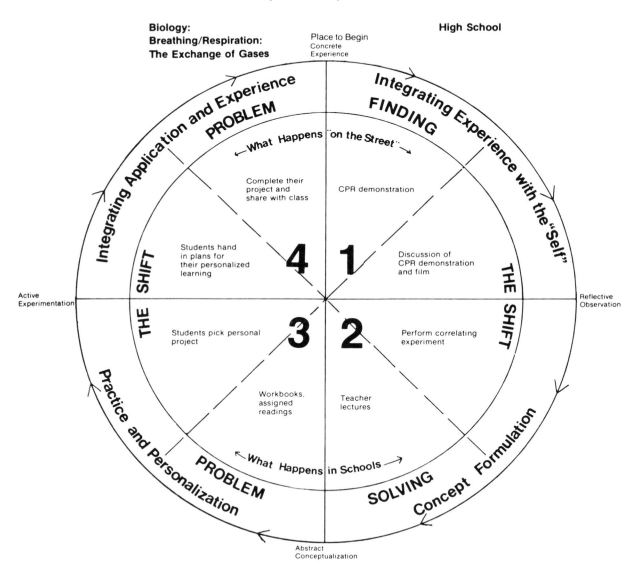

Biology:
Breathing/Respiration:
The Exchange of Gases

High School

Place to Begin
Concrete
Experience

Integrating Application and Experience
PROBLEM

Integrating Experience with the "Self"
FINDING

←What Happens on the Street→

Complete their
project and
share with class

CPR demonstration

Students hand
in plans for
their personalized
learning

4 **1**

Discussion of
CPR demonstration
and film

THE SHIFT

THE SHIFT

Active
Experimentation

Reflective
Observation

Students pick personal
project

3 **2**

Perform correlating
experiment

THE SHIFT

Workbooks,
assigned
readings

Teacher
lectures

Practice and Personalization
PROBLEM

←What Happens in Schools→

SOLVING

Concept Formulation

Abstract
Conceptualization

Footnotes

Introduction, Revised

1. Lieberman, Marcus G., An Evaluation of The 4MAT Project in Six Boston Public High Schools, Wellesley, MA: Responsive Methodology. July, 1986.

   Warren, Linda and David Dikter, An Evaluation of The 4MAT Training Project of Hamilton-Wenham, Ipswich, and Lynnfield Public School Systems. Hamilton, MA, October, 1986. (Both reports are available from the Excel Office, Barrington, IL 60010.)

Introduction, Original

1. The McCarthy Conference was held in December of 1979 in Chicago, under the joint sponsorship of McDonald's Hamburgers of Oak Brook, Illinois and Northwestern University of Evanston, Illinois.

PART ONE: LEARNING STYLES

Chapter One

1. Kolb, David A., Irwin M. Rubin and James M. McIntyre, *Organizational Psychology: an Experiential Approach,* 3d. ed., New Jersey: Prentice-Hall, 1979.

Chapter Two

1. Kolb, David A., Irwin M. Rubin and James M. McIntyre, *Organizational Psychology: A Book of Readings,* 2d ed., New Jersey: Prentice-Hall, 1974, pp. 27-42.

2. Kolb, David A., *Experiential Learning: Experience as the Source of Learning and Development.* Englewood Cliffs, New Jersey: Prentice-Hall. 1983.

3. Jung, Carl G., *Psychological Types,* New Jersey: Princeton University Press, Bollingen Series, 1976, p. 160.

4. Lawrence, Gordon, *People Types and Tiger Stripes: A Practical Guide to Learning Styles,* 2d ed., Florida: Gainesville Center for Applications of Psychological Types, Inc., 1982.

5. Simon, Anita and Claudia Byram, *You've Got to Reach 'Em to Teach 'Em,* Texas: TA Press, 1977.

6. Gregorc, Anthony F., Learning/Teaching Styles: Their Nature and Effects, *Student Learning Styles: Diagnosing and Prescribing Programs,* Reston, VA: National Association of Secondary School Principals, 1979.

7. Merrill, David W. and Roger H. Reid, *Style Awareness Text,* Denver: Personnel Predictions and Research, Inc., The Tracom Corporation, 1976.

8. Hunt, Valerie, Movement Behavior, A Model for Action, *Quest,* National Association for Physical Education of College Women, Monograph #2, Spring Issue, April, 1964, pp. 69-91.

9. McCarthy, Bernice, *Learning Styles: Identification and Matching Teaching Formats,* Unpublished doctoral dissertation, Northwestern University, 1979.

Chapter Four

1. *Piaget, Jean, and B. Inhelder, The Psychology of the Child,* New York: Basic Books, 1969.

2. Hart, Leslie A., *Human Brain, Human Learning,* New York: Longman, 1983. pp. 36-40.

3. Kegan, Robert, *The Evolving Self: Problem and Process in Human Development,* Massachusetts: Harvard University Press, 1982.

4. Ibid.

5. Ibid.

PART TWO RIGHT AND LEFT BRAIN PROCESSING

Chapter Five

1. Sperry, Roger W., Lateral Specialization of Cerebral Function in the Surgically Separated Hemispheres, *The Psychophysiology of Thinking,* ed. F. J. McGuigan and R. A. Schoonover, New York: Academic Press, 1973.

2. Bogen, Joseph E., Some Educational Aspects of Hemispheric Specialization, *USCA Educator 17,* 1975, pp. 24-32.

3. Levy, Jerre, Cerebral Asymmetry and the Psychology of Man, *The Brain and Psychology,* ed. M. Wittrock, New York: Academic Press, 1980.

4. Ibid.

5. Sperry, op. cit.

6. Bogen, op. cit.

7. Edwards, Betty, from remarks made at McCarthy Conference, Dec. 1979. The term "right and left mode" originated with Dr. Edwards in her book *Drawing on the Right Side of the Brain.* (See Bibliography.)

8. Bruner, Jerome S., *On Knowing: Essays for the Left Hand.* New York: Atheneum, 1966.

9. Bogen, op. cit.

10. *Brain/Mind Bulletin.* P.O. Box 42211, Los Angeles, California 90042.

Chapter Six

1. Kolb, David A., *The Learning Style Inventory.* Boston, MA: McBer and Company, 1981, 1985.

2. McCarthy, Bernice, *The Hemispheric Mode Indicator.* Barrington, IL: Excel, Inc., 1986.

3. Kolb, David A., and Donald M. Wolfe. Career Development, Personal Growth and Experiential Learning. *Organizational Psychology: A Book of Readings* by Kolb, Rubin and McIntyre. Third Edition, New Jersey: Prentice-Hall. 1979, pp. 535-563.

4. Ibid.

5. Edwards, Betty. Remarks made at McCarthy Conference, December, 1979.

6. Barbe, Walter B. and Raymond H. Swassing, *Teaching Through Modality Strengths: Concepts and Practices.* Columbus, OH: Zaner-Bloser, 1979.

7. Torrance, E. Paul and Saburo Sato, Differences in Japanese and United States Styles of Thinking. *Creative Child and Adult Quarterly.* 4, 1979, pp. 145-151.
   See also Ramiriz, M. and A. Castaneda, *Cultural Democracy, Bicognitive Development, and Education.* New York: Academic Press, 1974.

PART THREE

Chapter Seven

1. Suzuki, Shinichi, *Nurtured by Love: A New Approach to Education,* New York: Exposition Press, 1969.

PART THREE: THE COMPLETE MODEL

Chapter Seven

1. Suzuki, Shinichi, *Nurtured by Love: A New Approach to Education,* New York: Exposition Press, 1969.

2. Maslow, Abraham H., *Toward a Psychology of Being,* 2nd. ed., New York: Van Nostrand Reinhold Company, 1968, Chap. 4.

3. Bogen, Joseph, Concept of teaching used by Dr. Bogen and discussed at McCarthy Conference.

4. *Poetry Lives,* Orange Level, Evanston, Illinois: McDougal, Littell and Co., 1975.

5. Maslow, op. cit.

6. Maslow, op. cit.

7. Barbe and Swassing, op. cit.

PART FOUR: SAMPLE LESSONS

1. Hans G. Furth, *Piaget for Teachers,* New Jersey: Prentice Hall, 1970, pp. 85-104.

2. William Gibson, *The Miracle Worker,* New York: Alfred A. Knopf, 1957.

3. Clare B. Sullivan, former Reading Specialist, Fairfax County Public Schools, Fairfax, Virginia, 1981.

4. James P. Barufaldi, George T. Ladd and Alice Johnson Moses, *Health Science Series* Lexington, Massachusetts: D. C. Heath and Company, 1981.

5. Ibid., Level 1, *"Providing insects can smell," "Observing ants in the classroom".*

6. *Grace Nash, Music with Children,* Series I, Scottsville, Arizona: Nash Publications. See also *Today with Music,* Sherman Oaks, California: Alfred Publishing, 1973.

7. Herrmann, Ned, Former Manager of Education, General Electric Company. Currently Director of Applied Creative Services, Lake Lure, North Carolina 28746.

8. Harold R. Jacobs, *Mathematics: A Human Endeavor,* Teacher's Guide, San Francisco: W. H. Freeman, 1971, pp. 89-90.

9. Ibid., p. 90.

10. Marilyn Burns and Martha Hairston, *I Hate Mathematics,* Boston: Little, Brown and Company, 1975, p. 111.

11. Joseph L. Becker and Robert E. Kilburn, *Exploring Physical Science,* 4th ed. *Record Book,* Teacher's Edition, Boston: Allyn and Bacon, Inc., 1981, pp. 303, 304, and 342.

12. *Health Science Series,* op. cit., Level IV.

13. *BSCS Biology,* Blue Version, 3rd ed. Boston: Houghton Mifflin Company, 1977.

Bibliography

Adler, A., *The Individual Psychology of Alfred Adler,* Heinz and Rowena Ansbacher (Eds), New York: Basic Books, 1956.

Barbe, Walter B., and Swassing, Raymond H. *Teaching Through Modality Strengths Concepts and Practices.* Columbus, Ohio: Zaner-Bloser, 1979.

Berquist, J. W. The Use of Computers in Educating Both Halves of the Brain. *Proceedings: Eighth Annual Seminar For Directors of Academic Computational Services,* August, 1977

Bogen, Joseph E. The Other Side of the Brain: *An Appositional Mind. Bulletin of the Los Angeles Neurological Societies,,* 34, July 1969.

Bogen, Joseph E. Some Educational Aspects of Hemispheric Specialization. *UCLA Educator,* 34. 1975.

Bogen, J. E., R. DeZure, W. D. Tenhouten, and J. F. Marsh. The Other Side of the Brain IV. The A/P Ratio. *Bulletin of the Los Angeles Neurological Societies,* Vol. 37, No. 2, April 1972.

Bogen, J. E. and Gordon, H. W. Musical Tests for Functional Lateralization with Intracartoid Amobarbetal. *Nature,* 230, 1971, pp. 524-525.

Bradshaw, John L. and Nettleton, Norman C. *Human Cerebral Asymmetry.* Englewood Cliffs, New Jersey: Prentice-Hall, Inc., 1983.

Bruner, Jerome S. *The Process of Education.* Cambridge, Massachusetts: Harvard University Press, 1960.

Bruner, Jerome S. *On Knowing: Essays for the Left Hand.* New York: Atheneum, 1966.

Cutting, J. E. Sign Language and Spoken Language. *Nature,* 284, 1980, pp. 661-662.

De Bono, Edward. *Lateral Thinking.* New York: Harper and Row, 1970.

Edwards, Betty. *Drawing on the Right Side of the Brain: A Course in Enhancing Creativity and Artistic Confidence.* Los Angeles: J. P. Tarcher, Inc., 1979. Distributed by St. Martin's Press, New York.

Edwards, Betty. *Drawing on the Artist Within.* New York, Simon and Schuster, 1986.

Eisner, Elliot. *The Educational Imagination.* New York: Macmillan, 1979.

Eisner, Eliott. *Cognition and Curriculum: A Basis for Deciding What to Teach.* New York: Longman, Inc., 1982.

Ferguson, Marilyn. *The Aquarian Conspiracy.* Los Angeles, California: J. P. Tarcher, 1980.

Furth, Hans G. *Piaget for Teachers.* Englewood Cliffs, New Jersey: Prentice-Hall, 1970.

Gardner, Howard. What We Know (and don't know) About the Two Halves of the Brain. *Harvard Magazine,* March-April, 1978.

Gardner, Howard. *Frames of Mind, The Theory of Multiple Intelligences.* New York: Basic Books, Inc., 1983.

Gordon, H. W. Auditory Specialization of the Right and Left Hemispheres, in Hemispheric Disconnection and Cerebral Function, M. Kinsbourne and W. L. Sith, eds. Springfield, Illinois: Charles C. Thomas, 1974.

Hunt, Morton. *The Universe Within.* New York: Simon and Schuster, 1982.

Hunt, Valerie. Movement Behavior: A Model for Action, *Quest,* National Association for Physical Education of College Women, Monograph #2, Spring Issue, April, 1964.

Jones, Richard E. *Fantasy and Feeling in Education.* New York: New York University Press, 1968.

Jung, Carl G. *Psychological Types.* New Jersey: Princeton University Press, Bollingen Series, 1976.

Kegan, Robert. *The Evolving Self: Problem and Process in Human Development.* Cambridge, Massachusetts: Harvard University Press, 1982.

Kirby, Patricia. *Cognitive Self, Learning Style and Transfer Skill Acquisition.* Columbus, Ohio: The National Center for Research in Vocational Education, Ohio State University, 1979.

Kolb, David A. *Experiential Learning: Experience as the Source of Learning and Development.* Englewood Cliffs, New Jersey: Prentice-Hall, 1983.

Kretschmer, E. *Physique and Character,* New York: Harcourt Brace, 1925.

Lawrence, Gordon. *People Types and Tiger Stripes: A Practial Guide to Learning Styles,* 2nd ed., Gainesville, Florida: Center for Applications of Psychological Types, Inc., 1982.

Levy, Jerre. Cerebral Asymmetry and the Psychology of Man, in *The Brain and Psychology.,* ed. M. Whittock. New York: Academic Press, 1980.

Macmurray, John. *Reason and Emotion.* London: Faber and Faber Ltd., 1962.

Maslow, Abraham H. *Toward a Psychology of Being,* 2nd ed. New York: Van Nostrand Reinhold Company, 1968.

May, Rollo. The Courage to Create. New York: Norton and Company, 1975.

McCarthy, Bernice and Susan Leflar ed. *4MAT in Action.* Barrington, Illinois: Excel, Inc., 1983.

McCarthy, Bernice, Bob Samples and Bill Hammond. *4MAT and Science: Towards Wholeness in Science and Education.* Barrington, Illinois: Excel, Inc., 1985.

McCarthy, Bernice, Susan Leflar and Mary Colgan McNamara. *The 4MAT Workbook: Guided Practice in 4MAT Lesson and Unit Planning.* Barrington, Illinois: Excel, Inc. 1987.

McKim, R. *Experiences in Visual Thinking.* Monterey, California: Brooks/Cole Publishing, 1972.

Merrill, David W., and Roger H. Reid. *Personal Styles and Effective Performance.* Radnor, Pennsylvania: Chilton Book Company, 1981.

Moustakas, Clark. *Creativity and Conformity.* New York: D. Van Nostrand Company, 1967.

Myers, Isabel. *Gifts Differing.* Gainsville, Florida: Center for Applications of Psychological Types, 1981.

Nebes, R. D. Direct Examination of Cognitive Function in the Right and Left Hemispheres. In *Asymmetrical Function of the Brain,* ed. M. Kinsbourne. Cambridge, Massachusetts: Cambridge University Press, 1978.

Piaget, Jean, and Inhelder, B. *The Language and Thought of a Child.* New York: Meridian, 1955.

Ramiriz, M. and Castaneda, A. *Cultural Democracy, Bicognitive Development, and Education.* New York: Academic Press, 1974.

Rico, Gabriele Lusser. *Writing the Natural Way: Using Right-Brain Techniques to Release Your Expressive Powers.* Los Angeles, California: J. P. Tarcher, Inc., 1983.

Samples, Bob. The Metaphoric Mind: A Celebration of Creative Consciousness. Reading, Massachusetts: Addison-Wesley Publishing, 1976.

Samples, Bob. *Openmind, Wholemind: Parenting and Teaching Tomorrow's Children, Today.* Rolling Hills Estates, CA: Jalmar Press, 1987.

Simon, Anita and Bryam, Claudia. *You've Got to Reach 'Em to Teach 'Em.* Dallas, Texas: T. A. Press, 1977.

Sperry, Roger W. Lateral Specialization of Cerebral Function in the Surgically Separated Hemispheres in *The Psychophysiology of Thinking,* ed., F. J. McGuigan and R. A. Schoonover. New York: Academic Press, 1973.

Spranger, E. *Types of Men,* Halle, Niemeyer, Verlag. 1928.

Springer, Sally and Deutsch, George. *Left Brain, Right Brain.* San Francisco, California: W. H. Freeman and Company, 1980.

Suzuki, Shinichi. *Nurtured by Love: A New Approach to Education.* New York: Exposition Press, 1969.

Torrance, E. Paul. *The Search for Satori and Creativity.* Buffalo, New York: Creative Education Foundation, Inc., 1979.

Torrance, E. Paul and Sato, Saburo. Differences in Japanese and United States Styles of Thinking. *Creative Child and Adult Quarterly* 4, 1979.

Whitaker, M. A. and Ojemann, G. A. Lateralization of Higher Cortical Functions: A Critique. *Annals of the New York Academy of Sciences,* 1977, pp. 299 and 459-473.

Witelson, Sandra, F. *The Feminine Situation,* ed. E. Sullerot. New York: Doubleday, 1979.